NIGHT'S B EDOM FIELD MANUAL

CREDITS

PUBLISHER: CATHRIONA TOBIN

COPYEDITING: CHRISTOPHER SMITH ADAIR

AUTHORS: GARETH RYDER-HANRAHAN, KENNETH HITE

ADDITIONAL MATERIAL: GUMSHOE SYSTEM: ROBIN D. LAWS

ARTISTS: JESÚS BLONES, LUIGI CASTELLANI, RAINA KUPTZ, MARGARET ORGAN-KEAN, MIGUEL SANTOS, BIDDY SEIVENO, PATRICIA SMITH, JEFF STRAND

ART DIRECTION: GARETH RYDER-HANRAHAN, CATHRIONA TOBIN

INDEX: GARETH RYDER-HANRAHAN

COVER ART: DEAN ENGELHARDT

INTERIOR DESIGN & LAYOUT: AILEEN E. MILES

©2015 Pelgrane Press Ltd. All rights reserved. Night's Black Agents is a trademark of Pelgrane Press Ltd.

CONTENTS

Introduction ... 5

SECTION ONE: EDOM FIELD MANUAL

1000. E Squadron Special ... 7
Assignment — Level 1: HMS Proserpine
  Section 1 — Overview ... 7
  Section 2 — Duties ... 7
  Section 3 — Special Security ... 7
2000. E Squadron — Level 2: ... 8
Counterterrorism Operations
  Section 1 — Overview ... 8
  Section 2 — Operations ... 8
  Section 3 — Equipment ... 8
2100. E Squadron — Level 2: S-Serum ... 10
  Section 1 — Overview ... 10
  Section 2 — Use ... 10
  Section 3 — Benefits ... 10
  Section 4 — Side Effects & Interactions ... 10
2200. E Squadron — Level 2: SBA Escort ... 12
  Section 1 — Overview ... 12
  Section 2 — Transport ... 12
  Section 3 — Deployment ... 13
  Section 4 — Extraction ... 13
2300. E Squadron — Level 2: SBA Verification ... 14
  Section 1 — Overview ... 14
  Section 2 — Reconnaissance ... 14
  Section 3 — Authorisation ... 14
  Section 4 — SBA Deployment ... 15
  Section 5 — Verification ... 15
2400. E Squadron — Level 2: Field Precautions ... 16
Section 1 — Overview ... 16
  Section 2 — Bacterial Infections ... 16
  Section 3 — Symptoms in Humans ... 17
  Section 4 — Symptoms in Animals ... 18
  Section 5 — Symptoms in Plants ... 18
  Section 6 — Other Warning Signs ... 18
3000. E Squadron — Level 3: ... 19
Counter-SBA Operations
  Section 1 — Overview ... 19
  Section 2 — Indicators of SBA Activity ... 19
  Section 3 — Taxonomy ... 20
  Section 4 — Containment ... 21
  Section 5 — Termination ... 22
Research Operations Org Chart ... 23

SECTION TWO: EDOM PLAYERS' GUIDE

Edom Organization ... 25
  Director ... 25
  Scientific Adviser ... 25
  Military Adviser ... 25
  The Dukes of Edom ... 25
Edom Lexicon ... 26
Creating Edom Agents ... 28
  Vampirology, Edom Style ... 28
  Edom Tag-Team Tactical Benefits ... 29
  The Dukes of Edom ... 30
  Edom Cover ... 31
Bureaucracy and Edom ... 32
  Elvis (Alvah) ... 32
  Fort (Mibzar) ... 33
  Hound (Kenaz) ... 33
  Ian (Iram) ... 34
  Nails (Jetheth) ... 34
  Oakes (Elah) ... 34
  Osprey (Oholibamah) ... 35
  Pearl (Pinon) ... 35
  Prince (Magdiel) ... 35
  Tinman (Teman) ... 36
  Tyler (Timnah) ... 36
Edomite Equipment and Expedients ... 36
  Weapons ... 37
  Ultraviolet Weapons ... 38
  Tectonic Weapons ... 40
  Mirrored Sunglasses ... 42
  SBA Container ... 43
  Seward Serum ... 43
  Stake Tube ... 44
  Vampire Tester ... 45
  White Serum ... 45
Edom Tradecraft ... 46
  Special Edom Maneuvers ... 47
  Edom Tactical Fact-Finding Benefits ... 48
  Vampire Season ... 48
History of Edom ... 49
  1876-1893 ... 49
  1893-1894: Dracula ... 51
  1895-1917: a Thing of Shadows ... 51
  1917-1940: Preserving the Empire ... 52
  1940-1941: Edom Phase II ... 53
  1941-1951: Edom at War ... 53
  1945-1956: Hunting Monsters ... 54
  1956-1977: Edom in Shadow ... 54
  1977-1978: The Mole Hunt ... 55
  1978-1990: New Blood ... 55
  1990-2007: Return to Romania ... 55
  2007-Now: Project Montseir ... 56

SECTION THREE: DIRECTOR'S BRIEFING

BUILDING EDOM ... 58
  How Big Is Operation Edom? ... 58
  What's Edom's Standing in MI6? ... 59
  Is Edom Compromised? ... 60
  Does Edom Have a Vampire? ... 60
  What's Edom's Deal With Dracula? ... 61
Future-Proofing the Dossier ... 62
  The March of Time ... 62
  After the War on Terror ... 63
  European Politics ... 63
PEOPLE OF EDOM ... 63
Dukes of Edom ... 64
Scientific Staff ... 81
HMS Proserpine Ratings ... 86
Support Staff ... 90
Szohordoks ... 93
THE FIELDS OF EDOM ... 103
Hunting the Dossier ... 103
  Heat ... 104
The Opposition ... 104
The Oppyramid ... 105
  Row One: Surface Details ... 105
  Row Two: Digging ... 106
  Row Three: Strike ... 107
  Row Four: Chaos ... 107
  Row Five: Mortal Wounds ... 108
  Row Six: Destruction ... 108
Running the Campaign ... 108
  Use the Dukes ... 109
  Bury Secrets ... 109
  Edom by Day ... 110
  Prepare to Burn ... 110
  The Redemption of Edom ... 111
INDEX ... 112

EDOM FIELD MANUAL

Thy terribleness hath deceived thee, and the pride of thine heart, O thou that dwellest in the clefts of the rock, that holdest the height of the hill: though thou shouldest make thy nest as high as the eagle, I will bring thee down from thence, saith the LORD.
— Jeremiah 49:16, a prophecy concerning Edom

INTRODUCTION

This book is the *Edom Field Manual*, a companion to *The Dracula Dossier*.

The **E Squadron Briefing Documents** (pp. 7-22) are in-character files and procedures provided to new recruits, like Royal Navy ratings, officers transferred from the exoteric parts of British intelligence, or the petty criminals, defrocked priests, ex-Communist defectors, eccentric geologists, and descendants of certain family bloodlines that cluster around Edom like flies around a bloated corpse. If you're running an Edom-based campaign, you can give these documents to the players to get them in the right frame of mind.

If you're running a more conventional *Dracula Dossier* campaign, where the Agents aren't part of Operation Edom, then you can use the handouts as clues to be discovered in the course of play. Take down an Edom kill squad, and get their vampire-handling protocols. Break into the house at Ring, and get the Edom training manual.

The Director may photocopy these briefing documents as needed, leaking them to the players one document at a time. If a section or statement in them contradicts her campaign, or even reveals too much too soon, just leave out that page, or "redact" it with scissors or a thick black marker. Alternatively, just hand the players this book and hint darkly about the unpleasant fates that befall those who read beyond the approved sections.

The second section of this book, the **Edom Players' Guide** (pp. 25–56), is for players who intend to play Edom officers or ratings — either as undercover double agents (see *The Edom Agent*; **DH**, p. 29), as part of a *Fields of Edom* campaign frame (pp. 103–111), or in a whole new campaign of the Director's design that springboards off the Edom mythos but doesn't necessarily involve hunting Dracula. It's addressed to the players, not their characters.

The third section, the **Director's Briefing** (pp. 58–111), is all for the Director's eyes only. It's full of background information and advice on using Edom in your games.

Of course, since *The Dracula Dossier* is an improvised campaign, don't feel beholden to our alleged "canon." The history and structure of Edom described in this booklet isn't necessarily true — it might be what a low-ranking officer believes it to be, or what the CIA have pieced together over the years. HMS *Proserpine* may be an oil rig, or a shore station in Whitby. The real origin of vampires may in fact involve Satanic alchemy; perhaps Edom only clings to the notion of bacterial infection out of scientific superstition or as a cover story for skeptical readers.

There is no truth to be found here. Only a wilderness of mirrors, as paranoid, vampire-haunted James J. Angleton put it, and enemies that cast no reflections.

SECTION ONE: E SQUADRON BRIEFING DOCUMENTS

By opening this file you have become a prescribed person under Section 12(1) of the Official Secrets Act 1989. Its contents fall within the remit of Section 1 of the Act.

You have waived your right under the Armed Forces Act 2006 to elect for court martial. The Naval Discipline Act 1957 remains in force for E Squadron and associated prescribed personnel, including capital penalties for espionage and desertion.

1000. E SQUADRON SPECIAL ASSIGNMENT — LEVEL 1: HMS PROSERPINE

SECTION 1 — OVERVIEW

1011. OPERATION EDOM
Operation Edom is a joint operation between the Royal Navy Reserve Intelligence Branch and the Secret Intelligence Service's Research Operations Section through the Joint Forces Intelligence Group (JFIG), targeting bioterrorism threats to the security of the United Kingdom.

1012. E SQUADRON
E Squadron is a detachment of the Special Boat Service assigned to Operation Edom.

1013. HMS PROSERPINE
HMS Proserpine is the establishment where the naval elements of Operation Edom and E Squadron are stationed.

1014. ASSIGNMENT DURATION
The average tour of duty on HMS Proserpine is three months. If you qualify for Level 2 special assignments or higher, your tour may be extended commensurately. See Document 2000.

SECTION 2 — DUTIES

1021. MAINTENANCE AND SUPPLY
You will carry out maintenance duties on board HMS Proserpine as needed and directed. You will assist in supplying the station via helicopter or tender.

1022. SECURITY
You will protect and secure the station against intrusion, attack from within or without, or extreme weather.

1023. MEDICAL TESTING
All ratings assigned to HMS Proserpine are obliged to participate in medical and pharmaceutical testing.

1024. SPECIAL ASSIGNMENTS
Personnel assigned to HMS Proserpine may qualify for special assignments (level 2).

SECTION 3 — SPECIAL SECURITY

1031. PERSONAL HISTORY
Personnel assigned to HMS Proserpine are obliged to submit a full family history for genealogical research purposes.

1032. RESTRICTED ITEMS
All personal items brought on board HMS Proserpine must be submitted for examination. Items on the restricted list (e.g. mirrors) are not permitted on board and will be destroyed.

1033. PSYCHOLOGICAL ASSESSMENT
All personnel assigned to HMS Proserpine are obliged to undergo regular psychological screening and to keep a dream journal.

2000. E SQUADRON — LEVEL 2: COUNTERTERRORISM OPERATIONS

SECTION 1 — OVERVIEW

2011. ROLE
E Squadron provides tactical support to SIS/Research Ops as needed. The SIS/Research Ops Officer on the ground (DUKE) has operational command.

2012. THEATRES OF OPERATION
E Squadron may be deployed in support of SIS/Research Ops operations in any of the active theatres, in order of likelihood:
- Eastern Europe/Balkans
- United Kingdom
- Western Europe
- Middle East
- Rest of World

Deployments are usually covert; assets on the ground will arrange for local transport and support.

2013. PERMANENT ASSIGNMENT
In case of permanent assignment to E Squadron, you will be informed of special arrangements by your Training Management Officer.

SECTION 2 — OPERATIONS

2021. EXTRACTION
Covert rescue or recovery of SIS/Research Ops personnel or designated assets from danger. Extracted personnel may have been exposed to biological agents, in which case decontamination at HMS Proserpine or another approved site will be carried out by the unit Chaplain.

2022. RENDITION
Arrest of suspected terrorists or other persons of interest, and transfer to a holding & interrogation facility (e.g. HMS Proserpine, ABBEY, BLACK LIGHT). As per Research Ops operational directives, international law may be ignored in the execution of E Squadron missions.

2023. RETRIEVAL
Recovery of biological samples, documents, equipment, or other items, as directed by SIS/Research Ops Officers. Again, decontamination protocols must be observed.

2024. SURVEILLANCE
Covert surveillance/monitoring/interception (ELINT) of subjects designated by SIS/Research Ops.

2025. SBA VERIFICATION
See Document 2300.

2026. SBA ESCORT
See Document 2200.

2027. SUPPORT
Other support operations as tasked by SIS/Research Ops.

SECTION 3 — EQUIPMENT

2031. FIREARMS
For all shore missions, E Squadron personnel carry:
- Sig P229 Automatic Pistol or equivalent
- Special Issue Carbon Fibre Kukri knife
- Special Issue Tear Gas

- Special Issue Flashlight with UV Projector

When permitted by circumstance, personnel must also carry:
- C8 SFW/CQB Carbine or equivalent
- X-ATV-TR (see Document 2500).

2032. S-SERUM
All Level 2 Personnel must be qualified in the use of S-Serum (see Document 2100).

2033. DECONTAMINATION EQUIPMENT
Special decontamination equipment is assigned to qualified members of each squad. In extreme circumstances, you may be asked to employ or operate this special equipment without prior training. Follow the instructions of qualified operators without question.

2034. BIOHAZARD COUNTERMEASURES
S-Serum treatment and other precautions negate the need for GSRs or other safety equipment in most cases. All Level 2 personnel should review Document 2400.

2100. E SQUADRON — LEVEL 2: S-SERUM

SECTION 1 — OVERVIEW

2111. DESCRIPTION
S-Serum is a combat drug. All E Squadron personnel are issued syrettes containing S-Serum.

2112. MANUFACTURE
S-Serum is derived from human blood products. It is similar in function to the practice of 'blood doping' used by athletes. S-Serum is saturated with oxygen-carrying red blood cells and mixed with creatine and ephedrine.

2113. SAFETY
S-Serum has been in use for almost a century. Manufacturing limitations currently preclude the drug being made widely available to the Armed Forces. It is therefore restricted to E Squadron personnel.

2114. TACTICAL CONSIDERATIONS
As S-Serum's effects wear off quickly when the user is exposed to UV light or sunlight, S-Serum is best employed at night. If daytime use is unavoidable, all users should wear coveralls, face protection, balaclavas etc to minimize exposure and prolong the effects of the serum.

SECTION 2 — USE

2121. HOW SUPPLIED
S-Serum is supplied in 100 ml plastic syrettes, contained in a hard plastic case. A case may contain up to three syrettes.

2122. DOSAGE
A single dose of S-Serum is 100 ml. The effects of a dose last six hours on average (see paragraph 2143).

2123. ADMINISTRATION
Under most circumstances, your unit medic or Chaplain administers the serum en route to the mission site. If you are forced to administer the serum yourself, simply inject it into your thigh or arm.

SECTION 3 — BENEFITS

2131. COORDINATION
Considerably improved reaction time, hand-eye co-ordination, and agility.

2132. STRENGTH
Increased strength and endurance.

2133. PERCEPTION
Improved night vision and olfactory (smell) perception.

SECTION 4 — SIDE EFFECTS & INTERACTIONS

2141. EXISTING MEDICAL CONDITIONS
Medical clearance for E Squadron assignments also applies to the use of S-Serum.

2142. UNAPPROVED OR RECREATIONAL SUBSTANCES
Interactions between S-Serum and other drugs have not been scientifically studied; do not make use of any recreational substances, including alcohol, within 72 hours of using S-Serum.

2143. ULTRAVIOLET LIGHT OR SUNLIGHT
Direct exposure to ultraviolet light causes the S-Serum in the bloodstream to break down quickly, cancelling its effects within

a short time. If you avoid exposure to UV light or sunlight, a single dose of S-Serum can remain active for an extended period (up to 24 hours or more; it is not recommended to prolong the effects of S-Serum beyond 72 hours.)

Some users have developed a mild allergy to sunlight as a result of extended S-Serum usage.

2144. PSYCHOLOGICAL CONDITIONS

A higher incidence of schizophrenia has been correlated with the use of S-Serum. Report any perceptions of 'hearing voices' or other hallucinations immediately; if proper treatment is applied promptly, there are no lasting side effects.

2145. OTHER CONTRAINDICATIONS

Report any of the following conditions before using S-Serum:
- Received pre-Tridentine Roman Catholic Holy Communion (either species) within the last year
- Received Eastern Orthodox Holy Communion (either species) within the last year

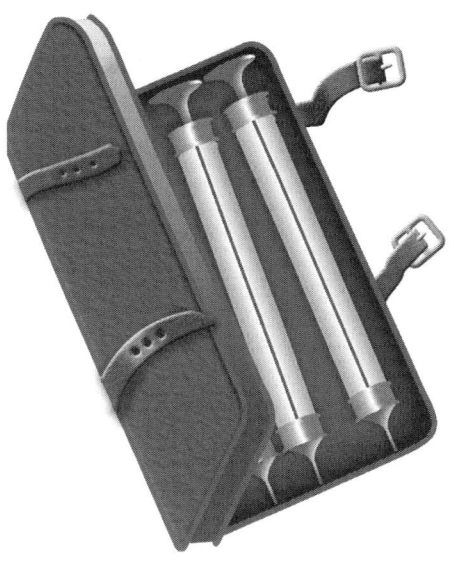

- Visited Romania or any of the surrounding countries within the last year
- Exposure to volcanic fumes or gas emissions
- Animal bites or unexplained wounds
- Recurring dreams or nightmares

MI.VI

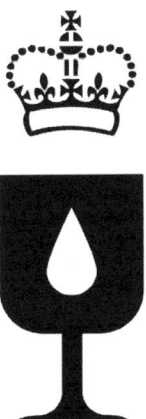

2200. E SQUADRON — LEVEL 2: SBA ESCORT

SECTION 1 — OVERVIEW

2211. SPECIAL BIOLOGICAL ASSETS
Special Biological Assets are precisely targeted biological weapons, designed to affect a single individual or small group of hostiles without risking infection or contamination of the surrounding area. They offer an alternative to UAV or covert 'wet work' operations, as the SBA can be released in the general vicinity of a target (within a town or other designated region) and allowed to 'home in' over time.

The existence and use of SBAs is classified TOP SECRET.

2212. SBA CONTAINERS
SBAs are deployed in Containers measuring approximately 450 cm x 1500 cm x 350 cm, weighing 300 kg.

2213. SBA ESCORT
The Container must be protected en route and brought safely to the target site. It must then be retrieved and returned to HMS Proserpine or another designated drop point.

2214. SUPPORT PERSONNEL
SBA Containers may be accompanied by SIS Officers or SBA Specialists. Follow any instructions given by SIS Officers. SBA Specialists are not in the chain of command; any interactions with them should go through the unit Chaplain or CO if an SIS Officer is not present.

2215. PACKETS
In addition to your SBA Container, you will be issued with three (3) packets, A, B, and C. Ensure that these are stored securely. Note that Packet A contains thermite. Packets B and C are not hazardous.

SECTION 2 — TRANSPORT

2221. RESTRICTIONS
SBA Containers may not be transported by air above 6,500 m and should be brought above

650 m only when absolutely necessary, due to the risk of anomalous weather patterns. Transport by road, rail, or sea is preferred.

SBA Containers must not be opened during transit. Unimpeded access to the SBA Container should be maintained wherever possible (do not stack or cover).

2222. CLASSIFICATION
If declared or questioned, SBA Containers are to be reported as containing agricultural chemicals, as permitted under EU REACH legislation.

2223. LONG HAUL
Any SBA Container transport with an estimated end-to-end duration of 48 hours or more requires special handling, and should be accompanied by personnel qualified under Document 2400. In the event of an unexpected delay when there are no qualified personnel available, open Packet C and follow the instructions contained therein to seal the SBA Container using the locking tools and other equipment. Do not approach the SBA Container once it is secure. Secure the SBA Container before sunset.

SECTION 3 — DEPLOYMENT

2231. OPERATIONAL COMMAND
Escorts are to defer to Verification-qualified SIS personnel or designated foreign allies on site in all matters relating to SBA Container deployment.

2232. PRE-APPROVED DEPLOYMENT SITE
In most cases, the deployment site has already been located and staked out by advance personnel on the ground. Secure the site, place the SBA Container in a safe place there, and remain on guard until you receive further orders or the SBA mission is verified.

2233. LOCATING DEPLOYMENT SITES
If a deployment site has not been located in advance, escort personnel must identify a suitable site. Such a site:

- Should be enclosed and easily defensible
- Should ideally be an old building, such as a church or mosque, but not one that is currently in active use as a place of worship
- Should be relatively isolated
- Should be near fresh water (lake, pond, canal), but not running water

2234. POST-DEPLOYMENT
Once the SBA Container is deployed, clear the immediate area. A thin mist or particulate haze may be visible shortly after deployment; this is harmless condensation and is not a biohazard. If properly handled, SBA weapons are lethal only to the intended targets.

2235. COLLECTION
Unless otherwise instructed, the SBA Container should remain in place for 72 hours or until the third dawn after deployment, whichever is longer. While SBA missions may be executed within a much briefer window, escort personnel should assume a 72-hour time to verification.

SECTION 4 — EXTRACTION

2241. EMERGENCY EXTRACTION
If the mission is aborted, escort personnel are to wait until the next dawn if possible before leaving with the SBA Container. If this is not possible, or if extraction of the Container is not feasible, then execute paragraph 2242.

2242. EMERGENCY TERMINATION
The SBA Container must be destroyed if it cannot be retrieved.

To safely destroy the Container:
- Open Packet C and secure the Container as instructed
- Open Packet A and spread the thermite evenly on top of the Container
- Light the thermite
- Douse the Container with the liquid in Packet B and withdraw

2300. E SQUADRON — LEVEL 2: SBA VERIFICATION

SECTION 1 — OVERVIEW

2311. PURPOSE
The purpose of SBA verification is to identify, monitor, eliminate, and confirm the elimination of terrorist threats using SBA weapons.

2312. TARGET SELECTION
Names of targets are chosen from a list curated by the Joint Terrorism Analysis Centre, with input from allies and trusted partners.

2313. MISSION SCOPE
The aim of SBA verification is to:
- Confirm the presence of targets on the JTAC list
- Confirm that there is a sufficiently long window of operations for the SBA to be deployed and take effect before the target moves out of the locale
- Confirm the termination or subversion of the target

2314. SECONDARY MISSION GOALS
If possible, and only if the SBA and all friendly personnel are secure, mission scope may be widened to include:
- Capture of survivors for rendition and interrogation at Black Sites
- Recovery of intelligence (documents, laptops, mobile phones etc)
- Destruction of evidence (MIBZAR protocol)

SECTION 2 — RECONNAISSANCE

2321. INFILTRATION
Infiltration approach is determined by the locale. If the target is in a friendly or neutral nation, infiltration will be under suitable cover (diplomatic, civilian as agricultural sales, petrochemical/prospecting, geological research, journalistic). If the target is in an unfriendly or hostile region, covert infiltration with INCREMENT support is the preferred method.

2322. CONFIRMATION
Presence of target may be confirmed through:
- Direct observation/photography
- UAV/satellite surveillance through DIFC/NRO
- Analysis IMINT (objects/terrain in background of training videos, face recognition)
- Interception & triangulation of ELINT
- HUMINT obtained from agents/sources/informants
- Testimony from SUBV sources
- Inference from the above sources

2323. WINDOW DETERMINATION
SBA Containers are dispatched from HMS Proserpine or forward staging areas and are subject to special transport restrictions and operational requirements (see Document 2200). Rapid deployment of SBA Containers is not presently possible. Once the Container is deployed, SBAs may require up to 72 hours for full effect. Therefore, the optimum operational window must be at least 120 hours (5 days).

Shorter windows will be considered (see Section 2413), as will Subversion or Special Observation (SUNSET OVERTURE).

SECTION 3 — AUTHORISATION

2331. REQUEST FOR RELEASE
Once Reconnaissance is complete, SBA Verification submits a Request for Release to HQ. This Request specifies:
- Name or code of target

- Locale and any complicating factors
- Window of Opportunity and any complicating factors
- Estimate of hostile forces present
- Estimate of collateral damage
- Estimate of intelligence yield
- Desired outcome (TERM/SUBV etc)

2332. TRANSMISSION

Completed requests should be securely transmitted to HQ. GO/NOGO response may be expected within 8 hours, followed by deployment of SBA Container within 48 hours.

SECTION 4 — SBA DEPLOYMENT

2341. SBA TASKING

Before deployment, the SBA must be briefed on its task. Where possible, provide the SBA with a sample of the target's blood or a complete physical description. Maintain 2400 readiness at all times. Escalation to 3000 protocols is not permitted without prior authorisation from HQ.

2342. SPECIAL OBSERVATION

SBA enables the use of non-conventional surveillance and tracking of target (SUNSET OVERTURE). Target remains an active combatant. Special Observation tasking is feasible in all cases.

2343. SUBVERSION

SBA induces personality changes in the target, turning the target into an asset. Often accompanied by changes in behaviour (delusions, blood drinking, obsession with SBA, fear of mirrors or religious artefacts etc). Subversion is unreliable and may have unexpected side effects. Target remains an active combatant, but can be induced to subconsciously sabotage ongoing terrorist plots. Subversion may require longer or repeat exposure to SBA.

2344. TERMINATION

SBA eliminates target.

2345. N/A

Task depreciated in revised Document 2300.

2346. OTHER

Compliant SBAs may be tasked with other missions as required. Maintain 2400 readiness.

SECTION 5 — VERIFICATION

2351. VERIFICATION

After the SBA returns to its Container, verification of the deployment's outcome must be obtained. Proof such as:
- Photographs of terminated targets
- Remains of terminated targets
- Physical evidence of an attack
- Photographs or video of an attack
- Testimony from eye-witnesses
- Recordings or other ELINT
- Reports from reliable sources
- Inference from changes in terrorist behaviour or network activity

2352. CLEANUP

Any evidence connecting Edom or sponsors to the SBA deployment or any subsequent attacks or incidents must be erased.

The SBA must be returned to its Container, or else otherwise secured (Document 3000).

2353. EXFILTRATION

Securing post-SBA action intel and prisoners is more important than maintaining an existing cover identity. Exfiltration scenarios in order of likelihood are:
- Exit under existing cover
- Exit under alternate identity
- Extraction alongside SBA Container
- Covert extraction — pickup by INCREMENT at pre-arranged RV
- Collected intelligence should not be transported with the SBA Container. Use of a diplomatic bag, courier, or other indirect channel is preferred.

2400. E SQUADRON — LEVEL 2: FIELD PRECAUTIONS

SECTION 1 — OVERVIEW

2411. PURPOSE
The purpose of this document is to familiarize E Squadron personnel with the larger geo-political picture of SBA activity, how that translates to battlespace conditions, and how to protect themselves from infection.

2412. NON-UK SBA
Special Biological Assets (2211) are derived from an original subject located in northern Romania. Edom's SBAs were created from samples obtained via that subject. Other governments both allied and hostile may have stolen or independently created SBAs of their own.

2413. SBA DISTRIBUTION (STATE ACTORS)
Countries known or suspected of possessing SBA weapons and/or pursuing same:
- United States of America
- Russian Federation (possibly other ex-Soviet states)
- Federal Republic of Germany
- Republic of Turkey
- Romania
- Other suspected state actors/states with possible access to SBA material:
- People's Republic of China
- Republic of Ireland
- Argentine Republic
- Syria

2414. SBA DISTRIBUTION (NON-STATE ACTORS)
- Vatican
- Caldwell Foundation
- PKK (Kurdistan Workers' Party)
- Neo-Nazi groups
- Organised crime syndicates in Eastern Europe

2415. UNCONTROLLED SPECIAL BIOLOGICAL ASSETS (USBAS)
Other SBAs may be uncontrolled by any state.

'Nests' of SBAs may be the result of natural contagion or fallout from improperly verified SBA deployments (Document 2200). Nests have been recorded in:
- Romania
- Slovak Republic
- Bulgaria
- Iceland
- Iraq
- Austria
- Germany
- Republic of Ireland
- United Kingdom

SECTION 2 — BACTERIAL INFECTIONS

2421. SBA BACTERIA
The bacteria is a rare extremophile species, living deep underground in volcanic vents. It cannot survive on the surface except in a host organism or a suitable storage medium. Due to its rarity, it cannot be detected by standard medical blood work procedures.

2422. AVOIDING INFECTION
Avoid touching or consuming the blood or other bodily fluids of infected organisms.

If bitten or scratched, disinfect the wound and report the injury on return to base.

Type 4 or greater protection hampers essential field action and is not normally needed.

SECTION 3 — SYMPTOMS IN HUMANS

2431. INFECTION OF HUMANS
SBAs are infected human hosts, with extensive physiological and psychological symptoms. Secondary infections cause less pronounced symptoms.

2432. HAEMATOPHAGIA
Exposure to SBA infection causes a form of anaemia, causing infected subjects to crave, consume, or become obsessed with blood. Subjects are drawn to bleeding wounds, display heightened sensitivity to the smell of blood, and may even attempt to bite and suck blood from humans or animals. Infection may be diagnosed by deliberately spilling blood or opening a blood bag near a suspected victim. In advanced cases, simply mentioning blood or topics related to it (life, death, drinking) may elicit a response.

2433. PHOTOSENSITIVITY
Exposure to SBA infection causes acute sensitivity to bright lights, especially sunlight and ultraviolet light. All E Squadron personnel are issued with UV-flashlights or gun-mounted UV projectors to exploit this weakness.

2434. ALLERGIES
Exposure to SBA infection is correlated with allergies to garlic and other chemical compounds. This reaction can be used to dissuade or diagnose infected subjects.

2435. ENHANCED SPEED AND STRENGTH
SBA infection may have benefits similar to S-Serum use (Document 2100).

2436. DELUSIONS
Infected subjects often manifest psychotic behaviour, such as:
- Religious obsessions or dread
- Schizophrenia, hearing voices
- Obsessive-compulsive behaviour
- Cotard's syndrome
- Insensitivity to injury

SECTION 4 — SYMPTOMS IN ANIMALS

2441. INFECTION OF ANIMALS
Some animal species can also be infected. Potential hosts:
- Canines (wolves, dogs)
- Rats
- Bats
- Crows
- Certain insects, such as moths

As most species known to contract the infection are scavengers, the likely mode of transmission is the consumption of blood or dead flesh.

2442. UNUSUAL FLOCKING
Infected animals often gather in large groups and move in unusual ways. Look for any of the following anomalous behaviours:
- Nesting in large numbers, especially in an unlikely location (hundreds of bats in a single small suburban attack, packs of wolves gathering outside a vehicle, thousands of moths clustering on a single window)
- Circling or 'waiting' around a particular place
- Following straight lines
- Following power lines or other electromagnetic sources
- Any of these behaviours may indicate animal infection.

2443. 'WATCHING' BEHAVIOUR
Infected animals may also display a 'watching' or 'stalking' behaviour where they fixate on one individual. The animal follows and observes the targeted individual, as though obsessed or 'watching'. This symptom is correlated with a more severe infection and may indicate the close proximity of an SBA-infected human.

2444. INCREASED AGGRESSION
Infected animals display significantly reduced fear and are no longer dissuaded by the presence of humans, vehicles, loud noises, or predators.

SECTION 5 — SYMPTOMS IN PLANTS

2451. INFECTION IN PLANTS
Plants cannot become directly infected.

2452. BLIGHTS
The SBA infection may co-present with certain fungi and impede plant growth, resulting in patterns of rotting or blighted plants. Look for concentric circles, lines, or footprint-like patterns, or for unusual blights.

SECTION 6 — OTHER WARNING SIGNS

2461. EARTHQUAKES AND GEOPHYSICAL PHENOMENA
Any earth tremors, especially localised ones, should be reported immediately.

2462. OBSERVING WEATHER CONDITIONS
Instances of the following atmospheric phenomena show a statistical correlation with the presence of infected subjects. While obviously a sudden thunderstorm or a cloud of mist is not enough to diagnose a bacterial infection, encountering any of these phenomena warrants caution and increased alertness.

2463. LIST OF CORRELATED WEATHER CONDITIONS
A) Sudden ground mists or fog
B) Unseasonable thunderstorms
C) 'Will-o-the-wisp' blue lights or flames rising from the ground
D) Earth lights — whitish-blue lights in the sky appearing shortly before or during an earthquake

3000. E SQUADRON — LEVEL 3: COUNTER-SBA OPERATIONS

SECTION 1 — OVERVIEW

3011. PURPOSE
This document describes established tactics and best practises for action against hostile, uncontrolled, or rogue Special Biological Assets, subtype V.

3012. DISTRIBUTION
This document coded CHAPLAIN and DUKE only. Other personnel are not trained or prepared for the use of supernatural weapons, and should not be employed in engagements against SBAs unless no alternative courses of action are available. In such cases, qualified officers may direct such personnel in the use of the techniques described in this document.

3013. MYTHS, FOLK BELIEFS, AND THE HOLLYWOOD EFFECT
Stories about blood-drinking monsters are common to most cultures. The unexpected popularity of the redacted *Dracula* novel placed a large amount of information drawn from Edom's own field observations into the public domain. However, between the deliberate misinformation planted in *Dracula* and the century-plus of 'cultural drift', many Edom personnel have dangerous preconceptions about SBAs. When conducting field initiations, reiterate that SBAs are not:
- Destroyed by sunlight
- Obviously pale or monstrous
- Shiny, tortured, or in any way friendly or sympathetic
- Instantly destroyed in a puff of dust when staked

SECTION 2 — INDICATORS OF SBA ACTIVITY

3021. LOCAL WARNING SIGNS
- Telluric distortions (unusual magnetic fields, earthlights, blue gas jets)
- Unusual animal behaviour
- Unusual weather conditions
- Refer to Document 2400 for details.

3022. UNEXPLAINED BLOOD LOSS
The feeding cycle of SBAs depends primarily on the physical and chronological age of the specimen and its level of activity. Subject KING was observed to feed only once during a two-month span of light activity, but consumed up to seven victims during a month-long voyage to England. Medical reports of unexplained blood loss or symptoms resembling anaemia may indicate the presence of an SBA. Typical practice is for an SBA to establish networks of agents and contacts to secure their supply of blood and hide their presence; it is therefore vital to locate and eliminate newly-arrived or newly-created SBAs before they can secure their feeding grounds and conceal themselves.

It is possible for an SBA to sustain itself on bagged blood for several weeks; however, no captive SBA has survived for an extended period without regular live victims.

3023. UNEXPLAINED DEATHS
Deaths caused by SBA attacks are usually reported as:
- Tragic accidents
- Undetectable medical conditions (brain aneurysm, sudden heart failure)
- Suicide

SBAs experienced in avoiding detection may falsify evidence to support either of these false conclusions, such as deliberately targeting victims who suffer from a genuine medical condition (cancer, suicidal depression) or disposing of victim remains in such a way as to prevent autopsy or medical investigation (fire, car crash).

Attacks by less cautious or hungrier SBAs may be reported as:
- Animal attacks
- Murders
- Unexplainable deaths

While SBA infection can only be transferred by the 'baptism of blood', accidental infection is possible, especially if the victim struggled with the attacker. Any suspected SBA victim is therefore a potential SBA in their own right.

3024. UNUSUAL PSYCHOLOGICAL SYMPTOMS

The presence of SBAs triggers unusual behaviours in 'sensitive' individuals. While the precise mechanism of this trigger has yet to be determined, the correlation between SBA activity and psychological phenomena has been experimentally verified. Watch for:
- Compulsive behaviour
- Geophagy (earth- or soil-eating)
- Entomophagy (insect- or spider-eating)
- Zoophagy (live animal eating)
- Haemophagy (blood-eating)
- Agitation around sunset and sunrise
- Intermittent explosive disorder (unprovoked violence)
- Obsession with death, eternal life, and/or related religious imagery
- Unusual dreams
- Unusual lethargy or weakness

Those displaying such symptoms should be considered compromised, and suitable security measures are advised (garlic, sedation). The intensity of symptoms usually varies with proximity to the SBA.

SECTION 3 — TAXONOMY

SBAs are classified as follows:

3031. TAMED SBAS

SBAs under the control of Edom, as per handling protocols described in Document 2200. These SBAs should not be terminated without explicit authorisation; if one refuses to comply with its handler's instructions or deviates from the agreed mission plan, it should be induced to return home, not destroyed.

3032. FERAL SBAS

Recently created or awoken SBAs. Feral specimens may:
- Make opportunistic attacks when hungry
- Return to the same grave or tomb each day
- Act on the spur of the moment instead of planning their actions
- Behave in a confused, animalistic, or childlike manner

If not secured, regular feeding will restore the feral specimen's strength and intelligence, enabling it to make a safe lair for itself.

3033. LAIRED SBAS

SBAs that have a secure or hidden lair or nest (castle, safe house, sewer, hospital). A lair may contain multiple SBAs, and may be inaccessible or otherwise hazardous. Laired specimens:
- Have preferred hunting grounds near the lair
- May have a small number of mind-controlled servants or guards
- Are concerned primarily with their own feeding and survival needs
- May have several hidden coffins or other resting places near the primary lair

Over time, the reach of a laired specimen or group of specimens expands.

3034. SUBVERSIVE SBAS

SBAs that have established a large network of servants and other assets, including multiple lairs. Subversive SBAs should be considered extremely dangerous.

3035. OTHER SUBTYPES

Refer to OHOLIBAMAH/KENAZ and Scientific Section for special handling protocols.

SECTION 4 — CONTAINMENT

SBAs are capable of avoiding direct confrontations through a variety of means (conventional SERE, physical transmutation, inhuman speed, perceptual distortions). The SBA's range of action must be contained before it can be 'run to earth' and destroyed.

3041. DAYLIGHT ACTIVITY

SBAs are injured, impeded, or weakened by sunlight. All containment and termination operations should be carried out by daylight if possible, despite the obvious challenges in conducting covert activities by daylight. Employ UV projectors indoors or if forced to operate at night.

3042. DESTRUCTION OF RESTING PLACES

SBAs must rest regularly in a suitable bed of specialised soil (or a bed that has been prepared or denatured). Failure to do so causes physical degradation (accelerated aging, loss of strength, mental confusion).

This can be exploited using the long-established protocol of destroying all but one of the target's resting places, forcing it to retreat to that last refuge. Ferals typically have only a single resting place, but more established SBAs typically have multiple resting places.

If the target suspects that its resting places are under attack, it may retreat to a hidden position and lie low, waiting until the hunters move on before re-emerging. Therefore, if possible, resting places should be destroyed in rapid succession or even simultaneously, leaving the target no room to manoeuvre.

Targets familiar with Edom or folk hunting techniques are likely to conceal or disguise their resting places. The traditional coffin or box of earth is merely a convenient container; an SBA may sleep anywhere that has a bed of earth between it and the local soil.

3043. RESTRICTION OF FEEDING

SBAs do not usually need to feed regularly unless exerting themselves, so attempts to contain an SBA by denying it blood are futile. However, SBAs commonly fixate on a single victim or class of victims; if these preferred targets can be identified, it may be possible to use one as bait or to ambush the target as it feeds.

Laired or subversive SBAs typically have other methods of feeding beyond simply attacking random victims, such as:
- Keeping victims imprisoned until drained
- Consuming supplies from a blood bank
- Cultivating willing victims
- Luring victims to a secure venue
- Having servants kidnap and remove victims after feeding

3044. THREATS TO ASSETS

If the SBA cannot be attacked directly, it may still respond to threats to its assets. Identify the target's possessions and networks, then degrade them with:
- Freezing accounts
- Police search and seizure of property
- Arrest of servants
- Interception of communications traffic
- Increased police or military presence in known hunting grounds
- Increased numbers of mirrors, CCTV cameras, etc in known hunting grounds

3045. THREATS TO TARGET

The target may be able to avoid probing attacks and feints, but each such attack interrupts its plans and forces it to expend time and resources. Exploit this with:
- Fire and explosives — SBAs have little fear of guns, but instinctively flee from fire
- Geodetic or EM disruption using weapons systems PLINY or DONNER (MIBZAR/TEMAN clearance)
- Poisoning or culling of rats, bats, wild dogs, and other such creatures
- Digging up cemeteries and other likely resting places

Even attacks that are incapable of destroying or impeding the target may kill assets or servants.

3046. RESTRICTIONS ON FREE MOVEMENT

Some SBAs appear bound by unusual restrictions on their movement. These restrictions can be used to help contain the target.

Flowing Water: SBAs cannot move across flowing water of their own volition, but can be carried across in a vehicle. Disabling vehicles and incapacitating servants can therefore restrict the target's range of motion. The use of islands or watercraft as operating bases is recommended.

Altitude: While SBAs demonstrate control or influence over local weather patterns, this power is not absolute. Unnatural and unusually fierce storms form spontaneously when an SBA rises above an altitude of approximately 3,000 meters. SBAs cannot therefore use most commercial air travel.

SECTION 5 — TERMINATION

Termination requires DUKE-level sign-off. Do not terminate without express authorisation.

3051. SLEEPING TARGETS

During daylight, most SBAs are dormant or extremely lethargic, making them appear vulnerable. Even in this state, prepare for sudden violent responses or non-conventional attacks. Use a Stake Gun or hammer to drive home a wooden stake, then proceed to termination.

3052. ACTIVE TARGETS

SBAs are extremely tough and fast. They prefer to grapple or bite opponents, and usually try to close immediately.

Use a suitable barrier (fire, telluric discontinuity, UV floods) to prevent the target from closing; have a second squad standing by with kukris to counter attempts to close. Ultrasonic repellers should be deployed if the target is known to control animals.

If the use of firearms is permitted, define a kill box and fill that zone indiscriminately with automatic weapons fire to ensure multiple hits. Continue firing until the target drops.

If firearms are not an option, incapacitate the target with a staged accident (car crash, building collapse, terrorist bombing) and follow up quickly with a stake. If no other option presents itself, a four-person team trained for close protection and armed with fighting knives can restrain a feral SBA long enough for the rest of the squad to effectively disable it.

3053. TERMINATION

The traditional method is to drive a stake through the heart, then remove the SBA's head and fill the mouth with garlic, then burn the target.

Dusting the target with thermite and setting it alight suffices if pressed for time.

3054. DISPOSAL

If possible, any remains should be brought back in a sealed container for analysis by Scientific Section.

A sample should be collected in any event.

RESEARCH OPERATIONS ORG CHART

OFFICE OF THE DIRECTOR (D/RO)

DIRECTOR, RESEARCH OPERATIONS; REPORTS TO C/SS

MILITARY ADVISER (MA/RO)
MAJOR, ROYAL MARINES. LIAISES WITH UNITED KINGDOM SPECIAL FORCES COMMAND; OVERSEES COVERT MILITARY OPERATIONS AND COMMANDS E SQUADRON

SCIENTIFIC ADVISER (SA/RO)
OVERSEES ONGOING RESEARCH PROJECTS (S-SERUM, SBA CONTAINMENT AND DEVELOPMENT)

FIELD SECTION

KENAZ: DOMESTIC AND FRIENDLY (EU/UKUSA/NATO) OPERATIONS

ALVAH: INTERNATIONAL (FORMER SOVIET BLOC) OPERATIONS

TECHNICAL SECTION

MAGDIEL: SENIOR TECHNICAL OFFICER AND ELINT

MIBZAR: WEAPONS AND SPECIAL COUNTERMEASURES

TEMAN: SURVEILLANCE AND SPECIAL PROJECTS

SUPPORT SECTION

OHOLIBAMAH: SENIOR SUPPORT OFFICER AND LOGISTICS

ELAH: ARCHIVES AND INVESTIGATION

TIMNAH: POLITICAL AND MEDIA OVERSIGHT

PINON: ACQUISITIONS

JETHETH: RESOLUTIONS

IRAM: TRANSPORT

SECTION TWO: EDOM PLAYERS' GUIDE

Behold, he shall come up like a lion from the swelling of Jordan against the habitation of the strong: but I will suddenly make him run away from her: And who is a chosen man, that I may appoint over her? For who is like me? And who will appoint me the time? And who is that shepherd that will stand before me?

—— Jeremiah 49:19, a prophecy against Edom

For more than a century, the officers of Operation Edom have protected the world from the vampires. They studied the Un-Dead to corral and control them — and to kill that which cannot die. You can join their ranks, if you dare.

Be the chosen shepherds spoken of in prophecy.

Fight the real war in the real shadows.

Go through the mirror that casts no reflections.

Play as the good guys.

EDOM ORGANIZATION

Operation Edom is an ongoing mission of the Secret Intelligence Service (SIS), still better known by its old wartime moniker MI6. Edom's existence is codeword restricted; not even the Prime Minister necessarily knows the full parameters of what exists on paper as the Section for Research Operations.

DIRECTOR

At the top of the pyramid is "D." "King Doeg," the director. When Edom was wholly independent and able to steer its own course on the black seas of the British intelligence establishment, "D" ran the whole show. Now that Edom is, at least notionally, part of MI6, "D" reports to some shadowy committee at MI6 headquarters in Vauxhall Cross.

By custom, each "D" selects his or her successor, usually from the ranks of the senior Dukes.

SCIENTIFIC ADVISER

Edom's current scientific adviser is "Dr. Drawes," the head of the operation's vampire research section. The scientific adviser is second only to "D" on the organizational chart, but this is an honorary rank, and the scientific adviser is not usually consulted on operational matters. The adviser usually maintains a senior position in some prestigious university or other government research institution, and consults for Edom part time.

MILITARY ADVISER

Edom is an SIS operation. SIS doesn't have its own special forces section (for that matter, SIS officers aren't usually armed), so the ratings on HMS *Proserpine* are drawn from "the Increment," a section of the UK military special forces that provides covert operations support to the clandestine services. Edom's military wing is codenamed E Squadron.

Officially, there's a space for an external military adviser from the United Kingdom Special Forces (UKSF) command to oversee the use of E Squadron, but "D" has chosen not to refill the position since the last adviser retired in 2003. Instead, either Nails (p. 70) or the senior captain from E Squadron fulfills the responsibilities of this post — which means that E-Squadron oversees itself. And since all of E Squadron's captains are long-term members of the unit and therefore habitual Seward Serum users, "D" can expect full and unquestioning cooperation from his military advisers.

THE DUKES OF EDOM

Each of the 11 Dukes has his or her own fiefdom, a portfolio of duties and specializations, jealously guarded against encroachment by others. When Operation Edom was conceived, the original plan specified a 12-person team. Now, some of the Dukes have a few subordinates in their sections, swelling the ranks of the crew.

The senior Dukes are Kenaz, Alvah, Oholibamah, and Magdiel.

Kenaz and Alvah oversee field operations — they actually go out, handle agents, hunt vampires, and latterly dispatch vampires to assassinate terrorists. When they need to, they call upon the relevant specialist Duke in either the technical or support section for assistance.

The Technical Dukes, under Magdiel, handle nuts-and-bolts stuff — computer hacking, bugging, firebombing, and the like — as well as weird anti-vampire weapons and fringe science gadgets like earthquake machines.

Support covers Edom's archives and asset management, run by Elah and Oholibamah respectively, but also its troubleshooters. If Edom needs some politician's doubts assuaged, or a package moved covertly across Europe, or some troublesome burned spies to vanish, they call in one of their troubleshooter Dukes.

For most Edom personnel, everything revolves around the Dukes. The chief is a distant, unknowable figure, almost as mythical as Dracula. "Dr. Drawes" rarely leaves his laboratory. The military adviser, if he exists, is off shuttling between HMS *Prosperine* and UKSF's Whitehall HQ. The Dukes run the show.

NAMING DUKES

The **Director's Handbook** lists the Dukes of Edom on pages 50–53, describing both their biblical codenames and the jazzier modern nicknames, and advises that you can use whichever style you prefer. However, as this **Field Manual** goes into detail on Edom's history and internal operations, we're going to use the biblical names (Kenaz, Oholibamah, Mibzar, and so on) for the *position*, and the nickname (Hound, Osprey, Fort) for the *current holder*. So, for example, Elah is the post of Edom's archivist and investigator, while Oakes is the tired grey man who's running the archives right now.

EDOM LEXICON

Like any small, highly specialized institution, Edom has accreted its own peculiar jargon and slang. Not all of these terms are still in use, but obsolete terms have been included as they may come up in conversation with elderly or retired Edom personnel, or be found in documents.

Abbey: In Edom parlance, the Carfax safe house / black site.

Andrew, Code or **Condition:** An unsecured vampire is present on the premises.

Baptism: Given the vampiric baptism of blood — either to be turned into a vampire, or to be made subject to hypnotic influence and conditioning. Colloquially, coercion or blackmail.

Beyond, The: Transylvania. ("You for the Forest this time?" "No such luck, I'm for the Beyond.")

Bigsby: Proper execution of a vampire, from BGSB: Beheaded, Garlicked, Staked, and Burnt. (*"Give him his Bigsby."*) Often "the full Bigsby." (*"Make sure he gets the full Bigsby, 'cos I don't want him coming back, now."*)

Blood, The: Usually refers to Seward Serum, but can be used to describe any vampire-derived serum. To "take the blood" is to inject the serum. Compare *Jack*.

Brass, The: As a location, this refers to the mansion and estates at Ring (*DH*, p. 172), from "the brass ring." More generally, it is used for Edom's leadership.

Chain Home Deep: Edom seismic early-warning system (p. 46).

Chaplain: *E Squadron* member trained in supernatural warfare.

Crew: Edom's personnel, especially those fully initiated into the secret. To "join the crew" is to be recruited fully into Operation Edom. "Crew of Light" is also used, usually ironically.

Cup, Drink From the: To be initiated into the conspiracy on some level. This is less specific than *join the crew* — it might be applied equally to a new recruit joining Edom from SIS, or to the recruitment of a new *szohordok*. Also used, sometimes symbolically, to remind another person of their duty to the organization (*"You drank from the cup; you know what that entails"*).

Cup, Pass the: To pass on the burden of serving Edom by handing over the duty to someone younger. It can be used as a term for retirement (*"Old Johnson's passing the cup next year — he'll be sixty in December"*) or as a euphemism for death. It usually has connotations of an honorable or respectable fate.

Duke: One of Edom's senior officers, whose codenames are drawn from biblical sources. By tradition, references to transitions between Dukes are minimized, especially in writing, to give the impression of perfect continuity. There is always a Kenaz, a Magdiel, or an Elah in Edom.

E Squadron: Special forces personnel on long-term or permanent attachment to Edom.

Forest, The: Romania.

Groundskeepers (obsolete): Romanian Securitate.

Guest: A vampire in service to Edom.

House, The: Peter Hawkins' country house outside Exeter.

Increment: Special Air Service / Special Boat Service personnel seconded to Edom as "shell squads." Unlike *E Squadron* personnel, Increment assets aren't officially briefed on the existence of vampires or the purpose of Edom.

Indulgence: Permission to kill. To "issue an indulgence" is to order the execution of a target. To "verify an indulgence" is to confirm the kill. Compare *send to the stars*.

Irish Testament (also **Irish** or **testament** alone): Bram Stoker's novel, or the unredacted case notes he filed in 1895. More generally, any story given to the media to cover up an incident. (*"Do we have an approved testament for this operation?"*) Occasionally, any cover story. (*"That death certificate looked a little Irish, wouldn't you say?"*)

Jack: An Edom field operative, either the trusted subordinate of a *Duke*, or a veteran rating from the *Rig*. Also, someone who has taken (or habitually uses) Seward Serum.

Jacked: Currently injected with active Seward Serum. (*"Everybody jacked?"*)

Juicy: Bait for a vampire. (*"Devin, you'll be juicy; the rest of us will cover you."*)

Lamplighter: MI6 slang. Courier; dead-drop and safe-house tender; long-term and overseas surveillance expert.

Master: "D."

Murrays (obsolete, and sexist to boot, and God help you if you use it anywhere Hound can hear you): Edom's typing and filing pool; people cleared to work with Edom material, but who weren't part of the *crew*.

Nest: A vampire lair.

Poachers: Any third party operating in Romania, especially the suspected German or Russian vampire programs.

Project Montseir: Edom's ongoing project using vampires as deniable assassins in the War on Terror.

Rating: In Edom parlance, a member of *E Squadron*.

Research Operations: Edom's official designation in SIS org charts. Within Edom, it's used ironically. (*"What happened out there? Why are you covered in blood?" "Oh, you know. Fucking research operations."*)

Rig, The: HMS *Proserpine*.

SBA: Special Biological Asset; a vampire or other supernatural assassin.

SBA Container: A sealed coffin containing a vampire, usually labeled as a container for hazardous chemicals or biological waste. Often shortened to SBAC (pronounced "ess-back" or "sback").

Send to the Stars (obsolete): A more poetic version of *issue an indulgence*, used only by the most pious or dainty Dukes.

Shell Squad: External personnel from the *Increment* or from a civilian agency (MI5 / MI6 / Special Branch) brought in to provide field support for an Edom operation. Shell squad members are placed under the command of a qualified *rating* or *Duke*, and are unaware of any supernatural dimension to the operation.

Ship: Edom as an institution or ongoing operation — "D" might be said to steer the ship, the 1977 mole hunt threatened to sink the ship, and so forth. Compare *crew*.

SUBV: Someone who's been hypnotized or conditioned by a vampire. Originally short for "subverted," but pronounced "sub-vee." Compare *baptism*.

Szohordok: Hungarian for "word-bearer." Originally it was a term for an outdoors bench where gossip might be exchanged; Edom uses it for both informants and dead drops (or brush pass locations) in Romania and, by extension, England.

Table Knocking: Intelligence gained through hypnosis or psychic powers; also, analysis based on similarly unreliable sources. ("*Magdiel's report on Pakistan is full of table knocking.*")

CREATING EDOM AGENTS

Edom is still technically part of MI6, and recruits most of its officers from there. However, it also poaches staff from MI5, the special forces, and the private sector, and is... flexible when it comes to giving shelter to defectors and burned agents. Edom's used to working with the Un-Dead — it's not going to blink at employing an ex-KGB wet worker.

Build your Edom Agent using the standard rules, with one exception.

Bureaucracy becomes a General ability, not an Investigative one, as noted in *Martini, Straight Up* (**NBA**, p. 195). The other rules from that build may also apply, depending on the campaign mode and on the Director's discretion.

You may transfer up to 10 free points from Network into Bureaucracy if you wish, representing a greater investment in Edom's espionage apparatus as opposed to your own web of contacts.

You can spend experience points on Network, as long as you didn't attract Heat during the mission. Nobody respects loud "tradecraft."

VAMPIROLOGY, EDOM STYLE

Your knowledge of vampires is considerably more focused and accurate than that of the average burned spy.

Edom has been studying, dissecting, and analyzing vampires for a century, and has verified what works and what doesn't even when it doesn't understand the underlying natural or supernatural processes.

You've studied Edom's after-action reports and autopsies. You've read all the files, from Vambery's early observations in the Near East to the work done in Porton Down with electron microscopes and retroviral therapy. You've pierced the veil of myth and superstition with the cold knife of science. You know:

- something of the true nature of vampires in this campaign — are they supernatural monsters or the products of some weird mutation?
- the names, histories, hunting patterns, modus operandi, and powers of major known, individual vampires:

EDOM PLAYERS' GUIDE ■ CREATING EDOM AGENTS

Dracula, the Brides, Lucy Westenra, Carmilla; Báthory, Lilith, or Orlok if they exist in the campaign, etc.
- how to "profile" an unknown vampire, or identify a known SBA by examining their kill sites
- how to determine the relative age and strength of a vampire, and how to trace a vampire's lineage back to Dracula
- the signs of vampiric mental influence, and how to diagnose the degree and duration of any such influence
- which weapons, substances, or ritual acts are genuinely effective, and which are empty superstition
- how to safely prepare and use the Seward Serum

At least — you know what Edom knows about vampires. You and they can still be surprised.

An Agent with Edom training has a different take on Vampirology, just as a medievalist and an influential political journalist might both have History 2 but express it in different areas.

EDOM TAG-TEAM TACTICAL BENEFITS

As an Edom officer, you've been trained to deal with supernatural threats. You may take any three of the following Tag-Team Tactical Benefits for free. Remember, using a TTTB requires two Agents, a winger and a striker (see the rules in **NBA**, p. 110), so two characters must take the same TTTB to gain the benefits. Consult with your fellow players to decide which TTTBs best suit your team.

Reptile Fund (Accounting + Preparedness): You're on the inside — and that means dealing with budgets and receipts and civil service bean-counters. A little creative accounting ensures your team has the expensive gear needed to keep Britain safe.

No Maps of This Country (Data Recovery + Driving or Piloting): You've spent months poring over satellite photos, ordnance surveys, telluric charts, and medieval maps of the land beyond the forest. You know Romania from the air; its roads and mountains are as familiar to you as the veins and bones on the back of your hand.

Follow the Blur (Data Recovery + Surveillance): You have processed enough blurred or invisible vampire imagery to know a few tricks of your own: crosscutting to reveal "empty spots" in crowds, using thermal cameras to identify "cold haloes," back-engineering imaging software to highlight "missing shadows." The Surveillance gain from this TTTB *doubles* if the winger first plants her own cameras in the area with an Electronic Surveillance spend equal to her Data Recovery spend.

Seward's Notes (Diagnosis + Shrink): You're adept at spotting the telltale signs of vampire influence on the sensitive and vulnerable. You've studied the case notes on Renfield and others like him; you know what to look for.

Jolly Raleigh (Diagnosis + Weapons): You know just where the kukri should hit, and how hard, to behead someone with one blow.

Drink From the Cup (History + Stability): Reciting the long and storied history of Edom, almost like a litany, can reassure your comrades and rally their spirits. Pass the cup — or the hip flask — and remember you're not dead yet.

Train in Vein (Intimidation + Athletics): Fighting something faster and stronger than you requires grueling coaching in specialized exercise routines: half reps, half katas. At the end of the workout, you're ripped for ripping. Can also be used with Hand-to-Hand or Weapons; specify which TTTB you're buying. You can buy more than one version, of course.

Check to the King (Military Science + Hand-to-Hand): You've commanded shell squads before, and know how best to direct fighting men and women in battle with an inhuman and supernaturally dangerous foe. You know when to go for the stake, or the kukri — or when to retreat.

The Blood Is the Life (Pharmacy + Medic): You're trained in the use of the Seward Serum and other vampire-derived blood products, and know when it's appropriate to use a small injection of the serum (or titrate it in sports drink) to accelerate natural healing processes.

Juice Box (Reassurance + Infiltration, for surprise only): You know how to project the kind of nonthreatening "victim vibes" that vampires pick up on — all the better to set up your partner's surprise attack with the kukri or the stake.

King and Country (Tradecraft + Network): You know how to pull the strings and use Edom's rolls of contacts and informants to the fullest. If someone isn't willing to talk, you can remind them where the bodies are buried.

The Knowledge (Urban Survival + Driving, UK only): You know every backstreet and shortcut in London, Exeter, Whitby, and anywhere else that warrants Edom's special attention.

Something's Coming Miss Liza (Vampirology + Sense Trouble): The mind-deadening effect of a vampire's approach causes even hardened veterans to stumble foolishly at the crisis. By close briefing and mental prep work, you can focus a teammate's mind on the target. The name of this TTTB is an Edom mnemonic for Stink, Cold, Mist, Lights — the standard spoor of the approaching Un-Dead.

Footsteps of Dracula (Vampirology + Surveillance): Cameras don't work, and it's hard to even keep the *image* of one in your mind for long — to recognize the vampire's face, instead of recalling it as a terrifying shadow. Your training, though, allows you to spot vampires as they prowl through the throng and rush of humanity on the streets of London.

THE DUKES OF EDOM

As Edom's troubleshooting team, the Agents report to one of the Dukes. Each Agent must choose one of the following Dukes as an immediate superior. The Director will, of course, exploit your choice of supervisor later in the campaign to generate interdepartmental intrigue and paranoia.

The Director is even surer to do this if you choose a Duke not on this list as an immediate superior.

Alvah (Elvis): Balkans and Eastern European field operations supervisor. If you're going abroad into the former Soviet sphere (Poland, Baltic states, Czech Republic, Slovakia, Hungary, former Yugoslavia, Bulgaria, Ukraine, Moldova, Belarus, Russia, and Romania of course), then you're in Alvah's domain. Gain 1 point in Human Terrain.

Kenaz (Hound): UK and Western Europe field operations supervisor. Anything domestic or theoretically "friendly" is Kenaz's territory, including "old NATO," Ireland, Austria, Finland, Sweden, Switzerland, and the UKUSA nations (Australia, Canada, New Zealand, UK, USA). Kenaz and Alvah tussle bureaucratically over Poland, Slovenia, and the Czech Republic. Gain 1 point in Streetwise.

Oholibamah (Osprey): Analysis and facilities coordinator. Lamplighting and field support — anything that involves existing Edom facilities or assets needs Oholibamah's sign-off. Gain 1 point in Tradecraft.

Timnah (Tyler): Political liaison. If a situation threatens unwanted attention to Edom, then Timnah or one of his trusted subordinates intervenes. Gain 1 point in High Society.

🦅 If you're using the Trust rules, then you start with 1 or 2 free Trust (your choice) in your Duke.

EDOM COVER

In addition to your own go bag of fake passports and previous service litter, Edom supplies Cover for most missions. The Director provides a mission-specific Cover pool of (usually) 3 to 5 points per player per mission, the Agency Cover pool. Agents can spend "normal" Cover points on Agency Cover tests, and vice versa. But anything the Agents do using Agency Cover can be tracked by their agency. Agency Cover pools go away at the end of the mission, to be replaced by a new Agency Cover pool at the beginning of the next.

In **Mirror** mode, any time an Agent uses his Agency Cover pool, he gives his agency 1 Trust point.

BUREAUCRACY AND EDOM—

Agents of Edom can use the Bureaucracy General ability to call in support from Edom. Most requests must go through a particular Duke or their staff. Increase the listed Difficulties by +1 if the Agents do not work for that particular Duke, and by +2 if they're on the outs with that Duke. Increase Difficulty by an additional +2 (or worse) if the request puts the Duke's position or self at risk.

A spend of an appropriate Interpersonal ability (see the descriptions of individual Dukes on pages 64–79) may, at the Director's discretion, add to your Bureaucracy spend. The Director may require you to play out the scene in which you approach one of the dozen most dangerous humans in Britain and ask for an illegal favor.

CLARIFICATIONS

The **inside scoop** on a topic means getting unvarnished, accurate information, along with speculation, tenuous rumors, gossip, and work-in-progress. Spending a suitable Interpersonal ability (usually Flattery) or offering a concession means the Agents also get an unambiguous and truthful answer to one question of their choice, within reason.

Basic logistical support means the Duke takes care of basic essentials — a place to stay, travel documents, and a cover story, maybe the use of a car. If warranted, it also includes weapons and an emergency bug-out plan (*"If it all goes wrong, go to this address and ask for Sergei"*).

Access usually implies that the Duke stands over the Agents while they read the reports or talk to the informant. Only rarely, when the Duke trusts them or they offer a big favor in return, would the Agents get unfettered access.

ELVIS (ALVAH)

Operations in the Balkans (technically, anywhere east of the former Iron Curtain).

DIFFICULTY 3

- Get the inside scoop on events in Eastern Europe and the Balkans
- Basic logistical support (Cover 0, transport, and cheap hotel accommodation) in the area
- Access to reports from Alvah's informant network (szohordoks)
- Clean up minor Heat (1–2) with Romanian police

DIFFICULTY 5

- Use of a safe house
- Direct access to an informant
- Access to reports and case notes filed by Alvah
- Draw down Edom cash for unexpected expenses
- Introduction to a specialist of some sort (treat as a 2-point Network contact, but their loyalty is to Alvah, not the Agents)

DIFFICULTY 7

- Clean up major Heat (3+) with Romanian police or SRI/SIE
- Major logistical support (mercenaries, significant firepower)
- Access to sealed reports and case files
- Draw down large amounts of cash (counts as excessive funds; **NBA**, p. 95)
- Access to highly placed informants and agents in the Romanian government, SRI, mafia (or even the Conspiracy)

FORT (MIBZAR)

Explosives and incendiaries, with special emphasis on anti-vampire weapons.

DIFFICULTY 3
- Assistance when planning raids on vampire nests or other bang-and-burn jobs (counts as a 2-point Preparedness pool)
- Access to forensic seismology reports (tracks natural earthquakes, nuclear tests, earthquake machine uses, supernatural quakes)
- Outfit an Edom shell squad with explosives
- One extra allicin grenade per squad

DIFFICULTY 5
- Access to explosives, WP rounds (white phosphorus, or "warm person" in UKSF slang)
- Access to proven anti-vampire weapons (UV lamps, holy thermite)
- One extra allicin grenade per Agent
- Arrange for an official bang-and-burn job (car bomb, booby trap, vampire-nest burnout) — this may require clearance from superiors; certainly, it'll be on the record
- Forensic analysis of a fire or explosion
- Trace the origin of a particular sample of plastic explosive
- Match an explosive device's design to likely bomb-makers
- Clean up 1–2 Heat by destroying physical evidence

DIFFICULTY 7
- Use of the Edom earthquake machine
- Introduction to a black-market weapons dealer or bomb-maker
- Off-the-books bang-and-burn operation
- Access to an Edom weapons cache
- Access to experimental anti-vampire weapons (X-ATV Tasers (p. 38), UV dazzle laser (p. 39), UV-emitter bullets (*DT*, p. 76))

HOUND (KENAZ)

Field operations and targeting, liaison with other agencies.

DIFFICULTY 3
- Get the inside scoop on current geopolitical hot spots
- Introduction to local police or intelligence friendlies anywhere in Europe or US (counts as a 2-point Cop Talk pool or 1-point Network contact; Difficulty is +1 higher outside EU, UKUSA, or NATO member states)

DIFFICULTY 5
- Basic logistical support anywhere in the world
- Access to information from the CIA database (but not the database itself; requests go through her)
- Inside scoop on known terror threats
- Inside scoop on current Conspiracy activity
- Assistance in tracking a target (decrease Hot Lead by 2, if using the Manhunt rules; *DT*, p. 87)
- Clean up minor (1–2) Heat anywhere in the US or Europe, other than the UK and Romania

DIFFICULTY 7
- Introduction to informants (or vampire-controlled assets)
- Direct access to CIA files
- Inside scoop on the vampiric assassination program
- Clean up major (3+) Heat anywhere in Europe, UKUSA, or NATO other than the UK and Romania. She'll only be able to do this *once* in a campaign.

IAN (IRAM)

Vehicular transport and field support. Also, murdering people with cars.

DIFFICULTY 3
- Basic surveillance assistance (one or two watchers in a car, staking out a target)
- Inside scoop on criminal activity in London, Bucharest, or Moscow

DIFFICULTY 5
- Full-court surveillance on a target (shell squad, 6 point Surveillance pool)
- Drive an item or individual across Europe, avoiding pursuers, customs checks, and speed limits
- Arrange the extraction of a friendly from a dangerous situation
- Provide a high-powered vehicle (nitrous system, tinted anti-UV windows, fake number plates)
- Introduction to a criminal contact

DIFFICULTY 7
- Kidnapping or assassination (+2 Difficulty to keep it off the books)
- Arrange extraction from anywhere in Europe; Difficulty is equal to 3 + the current Heat on the Agents

NAILS (JETHETH)

Security and carrying out of indulgences, a.k.a. sanctioned murders.

DIFFICULTY 3
- Inside scoop on current affairs in Northern Ireland, especially organized crime

DIFFICULTY 5
- Introduction to ex-Republican paramilitary contacts
- Old IRA survival and evasion network assistance — reduces Heat by −2 in the UK
- Provide a cache of weapons, explosives, and other gear that cannot be connected to Edom or the British government (+1 Difficulty outside the UK, Ireland, or Romania)
- Sit there quietly while the Agents have a friendly chat with someone (gives a 3-point pool that can be spent on Intimidation, Interrogation, or Bullshit Detector)

DIFFICULTY 7
- Straight-up murder someone (+1 Difficulty if they've got bodyguards or significant security; +2 if it's an off-the-books favor as opposed to an official Edom indulgence)

OAKES (ELAH)

Case file analysis and cleanup.

DIFFICULTY 3
- Introduction to an academic specialist or consultant (treat as a 1-point Network contact with only Academic abilities)
- Assistance cleaning up a crime scene (prevents the gain of 1 Heat, if the cleanup crew gets there before the authorities)

DIFFICULTY 5
- Access to Edom files on vampires — not the family jewels, but the files that actually talk about vampires, as opposed to talking around the issue with references to Special Biological Assets or "foreign friends"
- Access to information from the CIA database (but not the database itself; requests go through him)
- Inside scoop on known terror threats
- Inside scoop on current Conspiracy activity
- Help with analysis (counts as a 3-point pool that can be spent on Accounting, Criminology, Research, Traffic Analysis, or Vampirology)

DIFFICULTY 7
- Access to sealed Edom files
- Inside scoop on Edom, especially the 1977 mole hunt

OSPREY (OHOLIBAMAH)
Intelligence synthesis and logistical support; head of lamplighters. Right hand to "D."

DIFFICULTY 3
- Logistical support inside mainland United Kingdom
- Inside scoop on any unusual events reported by Edom's spy networks or other sources (a.k.a. *"Hey, Director, throw us a lead to follow"*)

DIFFICULTY 5
- Draw down Edom cash for unexpected expenses
- Help with analysis (counts as a 3-point pool that can be spent on Accounting, Criminology, Research, Traffic Analysis, or Vampirology)
- Logistical support in Europe
- Loan of an NPC lamplighter for an official mission
- Access to active Edom files
- Inside scoop on the current disposition of "D," and Edom's standing in the larger intelligence community

DIFFICULTY 7
- Draw down large amounts of Edom cash (counts as excessive funds; *NBA*, p. 95)
- Access to sealed Edom files
- Loan of an NPC lamplighter for an unofficial mission

PEARL (PINON)
Acquisitions and retrieval.

DIFFICULTY 3
- Introduction to a friendly expert (treat as a free 1-point Network contact specializing in Archaeology, Art History, History, Human Terrain, Languages, Occult Studies, Forgery, or Electronic Surveillance)
- Off-the-books access to friendly institutions (British Library, British Museum, possibly the Caldwell Foundation museum, various private libraries specializing in the occult and/or Romania, Cambridge colleges)

DIFFICULTY 5
- "Recover" an item of significance to Edom from a secure but not hazardous location (private home, business, bank)
- Introductions to criminal or art-world contacts

DIFFICULTY 7
- "Recover" an item of significance to Edom from a secure and hazardous location (military base, foreign embassy, vampire-haunted castle)
- "Recover" an item not of significance to Edom (e.g., steal the incriminating evidence linking you to a crime)

PRINCE (MAGDIEL)
Computer security and hacking.

DIFFICULTY 3
- Access to rumors and potential leads culled from the Internet
- White-hat hacking and securing the Agent's computers (counts as a 3-point Digital Intrusion pool that can only be spent on contests to resist intrusion)
- One-shot hack into an unsecured system

DIFFICULTY 5
- One-shot hack into a secure system
- Pwn an unsecured system (ongoing access until they realize they're compromised, and maybe even afterwards)

- Crash nonessential civilian infrastructure (take down all traffic cameras in Bucharest, or all the networked seismic detectors in NIEP)

DIFFICULTY 7
- Pwn a secured system
- Crash essential civilian infrastructure (banking, utilities, telecommunications)
- One-shot hack into a very secure system

TINMAN (TEMAN)
Anti-vampire gear and special equipment.

DIFFICULTY 3
- Requisition equipment from Edom's stores (counts as a 3-point Preparedness pool for common spy gadgets or Edom standard issue weapons)
- Technical support (counts as a 3-point pool that can be spent on Driving, Explosive Devices, Mechanics, or Shooting)

DIFFICULTY 5
- Requisition a custom piece of equipment for one mission
- Extensive technical support (counts as a 5-point pool that can be spent on Driving, Explosive Devices, Mechanics, or Shooting)
- Access to experimental anti-vampire weapons (X-ATV Tasers (p. 112), UV dazzle laser (p. 39), UV-emitter bullets (*DT*, p. 76))

DIFFICULTY 7
- Get a unique artifact or piece of equipment (e.g., Harker Rosary (*DH*, p. 268) or Knife Set (*DH*, p. 272)) out of Edom's secure vaults (getting it out without anyone else knowing about it is +2 Difficulty)

TYLER (TIMNAH)
Close protection and political contacts.

DIFFICULTY 3
- Inside scoop on politics in the UK, USA, Japan, or EU
- Invitation to an exclusive event (opera, conference, state dinner) — counts as a 2-point High Society pool
- Introduction to a backbencher MP or senior civil servant
- Clean up minor (1–2 point) Heat in the UK

DIFFICULTY 5
- Inside scoop on breaking political news (or scandals that have been kept out of the media)
- Inside scoop on politics in China or Russia
- Invitation to an extremely exclusive event (private party, conference where things actually get established, private after-hours chat with key figures)
- Robust diplomatic credentials in the right field (a 5-point Cover attached to the British Foreign Office or similar — if you need to be a UN weapons inspector, he can sort you out)

DIFFICULTY 7
- Private, off-the-books meeting with a senior political figure (ministerial or permanent secretary level)
- Clean up major (3+) Heat in the UK once per campaign

EDOMITE EQUIPMENT AND EXPEDIENTS

Although British intelligence agents are famously under-budgeted and forced to sign in triplicate for so much as a single clip of 9mm ammunition, Edom has its own workarounds. Its connections to the UKSF through E Squadron mean a sufficient inventory of weapons, and a few piles of dusty Hapsburg gold coins invested in the 1920s went a long way to establishing black accounts (possibly in Burdett's; ***DH***, p. 143) that the Exchequer doesn't need to know about.

Edom Agents can thus be assumed to have steady funds (***NBA***, p. 95) for their "onscreen" operations at least, and to be outfitted with standard equipment for their abilities. Tactical earbuds (***NBA***, p. 97), flash-bang grenades (***NBA***, p. 97), and lockpick guns (***NBA***, p. 98) are available in any Edom inventory or arsenal.

Night vision optics (***NBA***, p. 100) are deprecated by Edom, as vampires are invisible in their imaging systems, but they are part of the British security state's inventory nonetheless.

As trained operatives with a century of institutional backing, the players should use Tactical Fact-Finding Benefits (***NBA***, p. 107) and Tag-Team Tactical Benefits (***NBA***, p. 110; and especially the Edom-specific TTTBs on page 29) wherever possible.

WEAPONS

Edom ratings carry standard Royal Marines loadout:
- LMT L85A2 assault rifle (5.56mm, +0) with underslung L123A3 grenade launcher capable of firing hawthorn stakes (+1, Near range)
- LMT L129A1 marksman rifle (7.62mm, +1); one sniper per squad
- Glock 17 (9mm, +1)

All firearms mount tactical UV lasers. Long arms have integral video cameras: if a target is blurry or invisible, or vanishes on camera, pull the trigger!

Edom field agents are issued Glock 17s, if issued any firearm. That's why it's always a good idea to keep a shotgun with a stake-firing grenade launcher in a handy cache somewhere.

CARBON-FIBER KUKRI

This replica of the famous Nepalese blade is machined from carbon-fiber materials and contains no metal. It's slightly blunter, lighter, and more flexible than a metal weapon, but still capable of chopping through bone in the hands of a skilled user (or, equally, chopping through the fingers of an unskilled user). It doesn't show up on metal detectors. Theoretically, it can also be used as an ad hoc stake by embedding it in the chest of a vampire (Called Shot to the heart at +3 Difficulty, and honestly, just do like Harker did and go for the neck instead).

CROSSBOW

Edom's standard crossbow is a carbon-fiber reverse crossbow with integrated UV scope, custom made for the organization. It's spec'ed to fire larger-than-average wooden bolts (+1 damage) that might work as a stake if you hit the vampire's heart dead on. The design is unique to Edom, although other vampire programs may employ similar high-tech weapons (and the Vatican's vampire hunters probably have a whole arsenal of medieval implements).

GO-BAR

Although one can wield it as a heavy club (+0) the go-bar is better used to open sealed or locked coffins in a hurry (1 round). It lowers the Difficulty by −3 on the **Athletics** test involved (without it, the Difficulty is 8 for a sealed coffin; 12 for a coffin bolted from the inside). After the first round of prying, subtract another 3 from the Difficulty.

Made of spark-free metal, with a matte-black finish, it can also be used to force doors off hinges, lever open tomb-sealing blocks, pry open metal cemetery or compound gates, and for other forced entry tasks. For really stubborn doors (and coffin lids), Edom doctrine prefers thermite to breaching rounds (***DT***, p. 76).

IR/E GRENADE

These gas grenades combine terephthalic-graphite particles, Monnex dry foam, and micro-pulverized brass fragments with aerosolized allicin (garlic essence) to create a thick smoke screen that is opaque to infrared and (ideally) harmful or at least repellent to vampires. Ultraviolet, however, penetrates IR/E smoke.

When thrown or fired from a grenade launcher, the IR/E releases a cloud of smoke lasting 4–6 rounds and covering an 8-meter radius. It completely blocks optical, IR, and (non-UV) laser sights; targets on either side are effectively concealed (+3 to Hit Threshold and to attempts to locate). In theory, vampires must make an Aberrance test at Difficulty 6 to enter the cloud.

The allicin in the grenade's reservoir becomes inert within a month (much sooner if kept in a warm place) so check those expiration dates before you load up in the armory. The inordinate expense and bother of continuously refilling grenades with a tricky biochemical keeps the number of IR/Es available on any given mission low: one per team.

X-ATV-TR

An experimental creation of Tinman's, the X-ATV-TR resembles a normal Taser rifle, but much bulkier and more heavily insulated. Very thick and heavy batteries (think car batteries by weight and encumbrance) connected to the stock by thick cables power the weapon and magnetize its ammunition load.

TASER International already sells a 12-gauge XREP round (eXtended Range Electro-muscular Projectile) delivering the Taser shock without wires connected to the gun. Instead, the round holds a battery attached to barbed electrodes. When the round hits, needles shoot out of the round on wires, ideally producing two contacts and completing the circuit. The XREP round is very expensive and technically illegal in Britain. British police forces have used XREP weapons without authorization; Edom has a stash of them in its arsenals as (so far ineffective) anti-Renfield ammo.

The X-ATV-TR fires a modified XREP round in 10-gauge with a much more powerful battery, magnetized and spun up just before firing to "ground out" the charge of a *Carpathian* telluric vampire. (Each geological environment, of course, has its own signature charge; a Styrian Alpine telluric vampire, for example, is different.) Against such a vampire, the X-ATV-TR round does +3 damage and paralyzes and de-powers the vampire as if staked for two rounds.

The X-ATV-TR must recharge its magnet for 3 rounds after firing, and has a maximum range of Near (spending Shooting for Extended Range does not apply). Given the bulk of the electromagnet and its power pack, it lowers the bearer's Hit Threshold by −1. On an unmodified roll of 1, it also acts as an EMP on any electronics on the bearer's person — smartphone, laser rangefinder, flash drives, etc.

Against a Renfield or purely human target, the X-ATV-TR does +1 damage and costs the target his next four actions. Buying off lost actions costs 4 Athletics, not 3 each. If the X-ATV-TR is hit by gunfire, the bearer takes two instances of this damage.

ULTRAVIOLET WEAPONS

Aim an ultraviolet light with **Shooting** if it's an issue, but reduce Hit Thresholds by −2 for the target *and the wielder*: you've got a bright light pointing right to you, after all. Once a vampire's caught in the light, it costs 1 point of **Shooting** per round to keep the light trained on a moving target. If the vampire uses vampiric speed or otherwise distracts the flashlight operator, then another **Shooting** test is needed to reacquire the target.

HOLY RELICS

Edom doesn't issue crucifixes, holy wafers, holy water, or other Papist superstition as standard to its officers. Why? Any or all of the following might be true:

They just don't work. You might get lucky and run into a vampire who recoils from the cross because he thinks he should, but that's about it. The accounts in *Dracula* were colored by Stoker's Gothic imaginings and Van Helsing's theological line of patter, but actually describe chemical weapons and scientific countermeasures.

They only work if they're older than the vampire, and Edom doesn't have that many 12th-century relics or priests trained in the pre-Tridentine rite laying around for everyday use.

"Dr. Drawes" and his team are heavily invested in the telluric-vampire theory, and argue that relying on primitive superstitions clouds the issue of the true nature of vampires. Relics might work, but you'll never get one of Edom's staunch materialists to admit it.

Relying on such things might expose Edom to infiltration by or pressure from the Vatican. There aren't that many priests who are qualified and capable of dealing with vampires who aren't also already connected to the Vatican vampire program (**DH**, p. 76) or possibly the CIA vampire program (**DH**, p. 76), given the CIA-Vatican intelligence alliance going back to the 1980s.

Even if Edom doesn't hand out crosses and clips of 9mm sacred ammo, that doesn't mean that individual HMS *Proserpine* ratings or even Dukes can't harbor their own private beliefs — or private arsenals. You know you can trust a man when he lets you borrow his crucifix on St. Andrew's Eve …

Ultraviolet lights:
- prevent lesser Dracula-style vampires from using their powers (or increases all Aberrance costs by 2)
- injure Orlok-style vampires who are vulnerable to sunlight
- cancel the effects of Seward Serum, just like sunlight
- have no effect on Dracula (or, if the Director feels generous, increase his Aberrance costs by 1)

For UV-emitting ammunition, which you're not cleared to know about, see **Double Tap**, page 76.

UV DAZZLE LASER

The UV dazzle laser emits a bright blue-violet light that works like a regular dazzle laser (**NBA**, p. 102) on humans.

On vampires, it annoys and distracts them: all Aberrance costs and enemies' Hit Thresholds increase by +2, and all other Difficulties by +1.

It may also injure Orlok-style vampires vulnerable to sunlight (−1 damage per round).

It is illegal for security forces in the UK to use dazzle lasers, so Edom only issues one per team, and only for top-priority, short-duration missions.

UV TACTICAL PROJECTOR

Proserpine ratings and other Edom security forces are issued with underslung ultraviolet projectors for their long arms. Plain-clothes officers and undercover teams must make do with ultraviolet flashlights disguised as conventional lights.

Both models of UV light can also be used as conventional, human-visible flashlights; a mode selector switch lets the operator choose between UV only, visible light, and both.

UV FLOOD LAMP

These are battery-operated flood lamps, about the size of a large hardback book. They have peel-off adhesive patches on the rear, allowing them to be quickly mounted in position. Activate by hitting the switch or with a remote control. A UV flood illuminates a large area (8 m × 8 m, about the size of a courtyard) with intense UV light.

TECTONIC WEAPONS

Real-world conspiracy theories about tectonic weapons insist it's possible to create artificial earthquakes through manipulation of the Earth's electromagnetic fields, or by exploiting natural resonance frequencies (quoting Tesla's claim that he could destroy the Empire State Building with "five pounds of air pressure"). The US and New Zealand genuinely did experiment during WWII with using vast quantities of conventional explosives to create artificial underwater earthquakes and tsunamis, in a research program called Project Seal.

More recent claims point to Soviet-era programs called Mercury and Volcano and the US High Frequency Active Auroral Research Program (HAARP) as secret tectonic manipulation programs, and every natural disaster of the last few decades from Iran to Haiti has been attributed to secret earthquake-weapons testing by wholly reliable and trustworthy sources on the Internet and/or talk radio. Project DRACULA (***DH***, p. 151) might be cover for another HAARP-style device run by Find Forever (***DH***, p. 76).

A full-fledged tectonic weapon of the sort described in those theories is arguably beyond the scope of **The Dracula Dossier** unless you're running an airport-thriller style game (***DH***, p. 320). After all, if you can take out a city on the far side of the planet with an undetectable, unstoppable subterranean death ray, Dracula suddenly isn't quite so impressive, and such a doomsday weapon is unlikely to be left in Edom's grubby hands. The write-ups in this section assume that Edom's earthquake weapons are smaller, short-range weapons comparable in effectiveness, portability, and utility to a conventional explosive.

EARTHQUAKE DEVICE (MAN-PORTABLE)

This is the 21st-century version of Tesla's original design (***DH***, p. 266). It's a cylindrical metal device with fold-out tripod legs, small enough to fit in a briefcase or trench coat pocket. One end of the cylinder is bare metal; the other is studded with controls and sockets for cables. Plant the bare end in the soil and connect a suitable power source — mains electricity or a car battery — and you can use it to monitor or manipulate local telluric currents. It takes around four hours for it to map the telluric patterns of the surrounding area out to its maximum range of about five kilometers. Hook up a laptop computer running Edom's custom software to view the results (you need **Geology** or **Data Recovery** to interpret them), and you can identify geophysical anomalies that might be vampire nests or buried treasures.

Leave the device running for a full day-night cycle, and it disrupts the telluric currents enough to disturb any vampires within range. It's the equivalent of broadcasting high-frequency noise. This increases the Difficulty of any Aberrance tests and the costs of Aberrance spends made by vampires within its area of effect by +1, and makes vampires hungry and more irritable, shaking them into activity.

If employed as a weapon, it can shake a small building or other fixed structure to

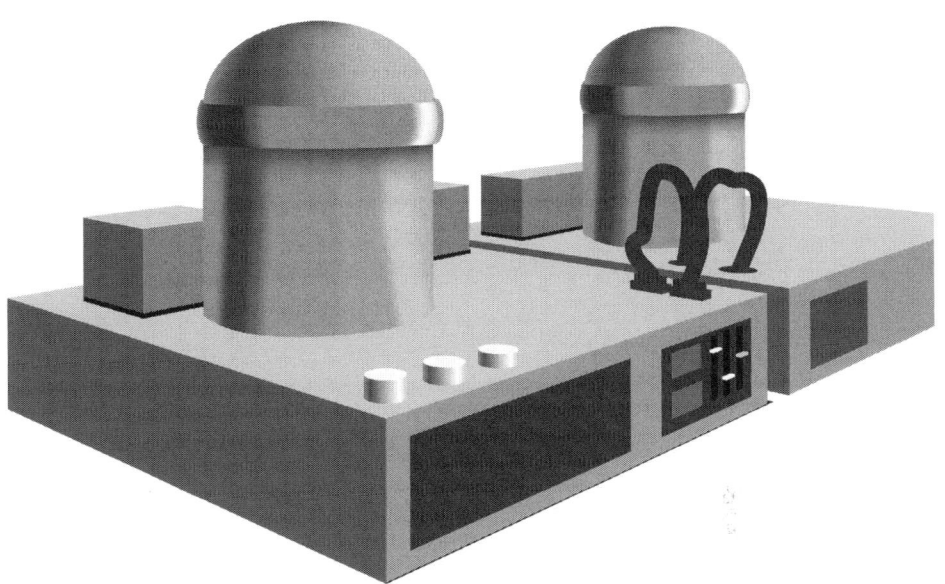

pieces, or cause underground structures to collapse — up to Class 3 on the *Earthquake Damage* table (p. 42).

EARTHQUAKE DEVICE (VEHICLE-MOUNTED)

This industrial-strength model resembles a portable generator, and can be mounted on a cargo truck or towed by a jeep or SUV. Edom keeps some in military camouflage, but also has a number of devices disguised as civil engineering vehicles for undercover use in urban areas. An integral diesel-fueled generator powers the device, although it can be connected up to mains power for extended use.

It works the same way as the man-portable model — it's just a lot louder and more powerful. It still takes four hours to map and profile the local telluric currents, but has a 30-kilometer range. When left running to disrupt vampires, it prevents them from sleeping peacefully. A few sleepless days are enough to give the unfortunate Un-Dead −2 to all actions as well as to increase the Difficulty of Aberrance tests and the cost of Aberrance spends by +2. The −2 penalty is lifted as soon as the vampire feeds — nothing like hot blood to renew youth and revitalize tired limbs. The Aberrance penalty, though, stays as long as the vampire remains within the generator's range of influence. The vampire can take steps to shield itself from the telluric dissonance — sleeping in the grave of a suicide, hiding a coffin high off the ground, or moving to a geologically sheltered spot.

When used as a weapon, the vehicle-mounted earthquake device can kick out enough of a quake to devastate a city. Again, the range for attacks is much shorter, on the order of a few hundred meters. The device can generate anything up to a Class 3 attack without problems. A Class 4 or 5 attack, even an unsuccessful one, damages the machine's internal workings enough to require repairs (**Mechanics**, Difficulty 6). A Class 6 attack tears the machine apart violently.

EARTHQUAKE DAMAGE

CLASS	EXAMPLES	COLLAPSE DAMAGE	DEBRIS RANGE	DEBRIS DAMAGE
1	Prefab building	+2	Point-Blank	−2
2	Small house, aging sewer, friable or stressed natural cave, volcanic vent	+3	Point-Blank	−1
3	Part of a block, subway or sewer, sea cave	+4	Close	+0
4	City block or large building, deep subway, natural cave	+6	Near	+1
5	Neighborhood	+6	Near	+2
6	Entire city, deep cavern	+8	Long	+3

USING EARTHQUAKE DEVICES

Calibrating and targeting an earthquake device requires a **Mechanics** test, at a Difficulty of 3 + the Class of destruction desired. Spending 2 points of **Geology** reduces the Difficulty by −1. By spending 1 point of **Geology** in a tectonically active zone, the operator can focus the device to trigger an existing earthquake fault and increase the damage by one Class "for free."

Operating the device in an avalanche zone risks triggering an avalanche (Class 4) regardless of setting; add +2 to Difficulty to avoid it.

If the test fails, the telluric energies might dissipate harmlessly, or cause a smaller unfocused earth tremor, or even trigger a larger unplanned natural earthquake or volcano. If the test succeeds, the device shakes the target structure to pieces.

Collapse Damage applies to Agents and significant NPCs caught in the collapsing building. (Mooks just die or get buried in rubble or landslides.) Agents near an exit (perhaps with an **Architecture** spend if it's in doubt) get to make an **Athletics** test with the earthquake's Class times 3 as the Difficulty.

If successful, they escape the building before it collapses, and take debris damage instead of collapse damage. If no exit is nearby, that **Athletics** test lets the character take shelter in time, reducing damage by 2.

Debris Range is the distance from the quake's epicenter at which falling masonry, broken glass, and other debris is still a major threat. Agents who escape a collapsing building, or who are simply near the site of a telluric attack, are at risk of debris damage. They may make an **Athletics** test with the earthquake's Class times 3 as the Difficulty. If successful, they take no damage; otherwise, they suffer the listed injury.

MIRRORED SUNGLASSES

IR- and UV-polarized, these mirror-surfaced sunglasses are completely incompatible with NVOs, laser scopes, and similar. But they are opaque to vampire vision, while presenting the vampire with a discomforting absence of its own image. The wearer can still see the vampire's eyes and thus remains susceptible to mesmerism or other mind control attempts. But between the mirror and the blankness, the wearer gets one round to make a **Sense Trouble** or **Stability** test at Difficulty 4 before the vampiric mind control can begin.

The world being a late William Gibson novel, not an early William Gibson novel, mirror shades are fairly conspicuous in the field (+1 to Difficulty of **Disguise** and **Surveillance** tests; +2 against anyone who might know what to look for).

SBA CONTAINER

"Coffin" isn't the first thing that springs to mind when you see one of these, and that's the idea. Special Biological Asset containers are designed to hide the vampire within, and resemble refrigerated canisters for biological samples or toxic waste, cocooned in a bewildering mess of valves, tubes, and warning labels. Unmarked intake valves allow handlers to pump in blood to feed the asset, and there's a storage tank that automatically dispenses a quantity of blood every day for long journeys. Pull one concealed lever to open up an exit valve, allowing a vampire to slip out of the container in mist form, or unscrew one end for direct access to the coffin compartment and its bed of native soil. If neither valve nor hatch is open, the coffin is hermetically sealed and secure.

Other useful features: an integral GPS tracker, a Bluetooth speaker inside the coffin so the handlers can speak with the monster without having to let it out. (Or play audio briefings in transit. Or audiobooks.)

On top of each SBA container, secured by a metal-aramid cable, is a locked box holding three large foil envelopes, marked A, B, and C.

Packet A contains plenty of thermite, possibly mixed in with ground fragments of the bones of a saint and/or meteorite dust. It's +2 damage for 2–12 rounds if you get covered in the stuff, and hopefully much more for a vampire.

Packet B is a liquid. Holy water, or a potent but short-lived antibacterial agent? Either way, the substance is designed to salt the earth where the vampire died, preventing it from rising again — and ensuring that no one else can recover anything useful from the remains. A chemical stake, if you will.

Packet C contains a putty-like substance doused in a reddish liquid. Instructions on the packet describe how the putty should be placed around the container to "secure the contents." It might be the Host, or it might be an extremely strong and airtight polymer-epoxy binary sealant capable of restraining a vampire in mist form.

SEWARD SERUM

Derived from a homeopathic distillation of vampire blood — or so the story goes — the Seward Serum is Edom's signature combat drug / substance abuse program. The drug may be issued as single-use syringes in a hard case, disguised as medication, or in ampoules for use with an injection gun when you need to dose a whole squad of Jacks in a hurry.

Injecting yourself takes your action; spend 2 points of **Medic** to combine it with another action.

After injection, you gain:

- 12 pool points to be distributed among any of the following General abilities: Athletics, Conceal, Digital Intrusion, Driving, Explosive Devices, Filch, Gambling, Hand-to-Hand, Health, Infiltration, Mechanics (traps only), Piloting, Preparedness, Sense Trouble, Shooting, Surveillance, Stability, or Weapons. You don't need to assign points straight away; you can hold them in reserve until you need 'em.
- Heightened senses — able to see in the dark (treat as vampiric Infravision), enhanced senses of taste and smell, better hearing. At the Director's

discretion, clues that normally require a Bullshit Detector or Notice spend are free while you're Jacked.
- +1 melee damage with Hand-to-Hand or Weapons.
- Vampiric Speed (spend 2 Athletics or Health for an Extra Attack, Jump In, Mook Shield, or +2 Hit Threshold for one round. You can only spend 2 Athletics per round on this power; you can spend Health multiple times, but the cost increases by +1 per extra use in a round).
- Slowed aging while under the effects of the serum.

The big weakness of the serum is that it's canceled by sunlight or direct UV light. If exposed to sunlight, you instantly lose any temporary points you added to your pools. This includes Health and Stability, which can be dropped into negative territory through abuse of Seward Serum. (For example, you've got 8 Health. You allocate 4 of your Seward Serum points to Health, bringing you to 12, and then eat a bullet, dropping you to 2 Health. You're then exposed to sunlight; your Seward Serum points vanish, including those spent on Health, so you lose another 4 Health, bringing you to −2 and Hurt.)

If you become Shaken (0 Stability or less) while under the effects of the serum, gain an Addictive Disorder (**NBA**, p. 84) to the serum.

You're at +1 to all Difficulties to resist Dracula (or vampiric compulsions in general, if the Director is feeling cruel).

The serum's only standard issue for E Squadron squaddies. Edom field officers like you need to spend **Preparedness** to have it to hand; it's Difficulty 2 if the brass expect trouble, Difficulty 4 for a routine mission, and Difficulty 5 to have some on you when you're off duty.

The serum must be stored carefully — exposure to sunlight ruins a dose almost instantly.

STAKE TUBE

This is one of Tinman's contraptions. Driving a stake through the ribcage is no easy feat — it's like driving a railroad

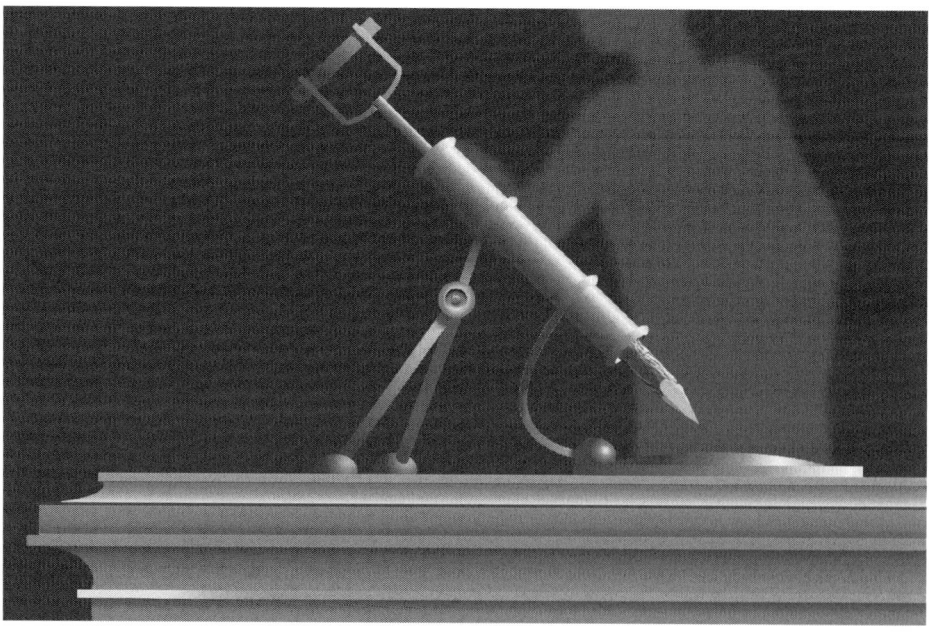

spike into the ground. It took a big man like Arthur Holmwood several blows with a hammer to stake Lucy Westenra; in the field, Edom officers don't always have the luxury of time.

The Stake Tube has a gas-powered piston that drives the stake down with great force, impaling a vampire in a single devastating thrust. It takes only a moment to set up: unclasp the extensible legs and position it above the vampire's chest, pull the yellow plastic ripcord, and stand back. You get one shot with it, so make it count.

While it's designed for use on sleeping vampires, the Stake Tube can be used as a short-range ... well, it's closer to a ballista than a crossbow, weapons nerds. Attack with Weapons at +1 Difficulty because it's so unwieldy, but it does +2 damage on a hit.

ULTRASONIC REPELLER

Press the button, and this little box screams a high-frequency noise that's barely perceptible to humans. Animals, though, find it intolerably painful. It works on rats, bats, dogs, and most other small creatures, incapacitating them for at least 1–3 rounds and driving them away after that. A vampire with the power to command such animals can rally the furry troops, but that costs 2 extra points of Aberrance. Ultrasonic repellers cause hearing loss in humans if used repeatedly (−1 to Sense Trouble after two uses in a session).

VAMPIRE TESTER

A handheld device about the size of a big remote control, the Vampire Tester works by projecting an intense burst of short-ranged UV light from an emitter at one end. A camera next to the projector looks for telltale changes in skin tone and texture caused by the vampiric reaction to UV light (assuming such a thing exists in your campaign). To use the device, simply hold it over a suspect's hand or face at short range and press the button. If the red light glows, you've probably found a vampire — or someone with extremely sensitive skin, anyway.

A successful **Filch** test (Difficulty of 5 + the target's Alertness Modifier) allows an Edom agent to test a subject without them noticing. The tester can be set to vibrate on a positive test instead of lighting up or beeping.

The tester is not infallible. Skin conditions and some types of makeup can give false positives, while a thick layer of protective sunscreen or other UV-absorbing substances can hide a vampire from the device. It only detects vampires, not Renfields or other supernatural creatures. However, it is cheap, portable, and can be used to quickly eliminate large numbers of suspects, which can be a boon in certain situations.

Using the Vampire Tester accurately requires a 1-point **Vampirology** or **Diagnosis** spend.

This device only works in campaigns where vampires routinely show up on camera or in other imagery (not the case in the default *Dracula Dossier* game), and in which UV affects them more than it does humans. (See *The Two-Way Mirror; NBA,* p. 131.)

WHITE SERUM

Another blood product, this serum makes the user's blood poisonous to vampires. For that matter, it makes the user's blood poisonous to the user — repeated use often leads to kidney or liver failure. Edom doctors may prescribe the serum to suspected vampire victims, to prevent further attacks. It may also be used to prepare bait for a hostile vampire.

The origin of the White Serum is unknown; it was obtained by Edom during the 1950s, possibly from the research conducted by the Caldwell Foundation. Supplies of the serum are extremely limited.

To humans, the serum behaves as a poison.

Onset: Sunset

Test: Difficulty 4 Health (+1 Difficulty per previous White Serum injection)

Minor: +2 damage over the next 2–12 hours

Severe: +4 damage, Hurt; 4-point Stability loss

If the user takes another similar serum, like the Seward Serum (p. 43) or Serum V (*DH*, p. 162), the effect of the other serum is canceled and the White Serum's effects are automatically severe.

If a vampire drinks the blood of a user, the effects are more dramatic. Use the values before the slash if the vampire simply bites the user; use the second set of values if the vampire actually feeds.

Onset: One round

Test: Difficulty 4 Health/Difficulty 8 Health

Minor: +0 damage/+2 damage

Severe: +2 damage/+4 damage; in either case, the vampire loses an equal number of points from its Aberrance pool.

EDOM TRADECRAFT

Edom is a century-old operation, with traditions and standards that predate strict modern tradecraft as such. While individual recognition codes and phrases change with each mission these days, every Edom agent with Tradecraft knows the old legendary ways, too. It's more common to see them used by survivors or successors of very old, possibly even forgotten, Edom asset networks. Of course, Edom's enemies might have also learned these old tradecrafty ways — because some of them were alive when they were the new ways.

The **"Edom flash"** or **"Edom blaze"** is a cup and a drop, based on the Edom logo. Cut into a tree's bark, drawn on a wall, scrawled on a sign, or in any sort of fashion, it means "Edom Was Here" or just "Check

CHAIN HOME DEEP

The original Chain Home (CH) network of early-warning radar stations was built during World War II to detect approaching German bombers. It was supplemented with the more advanced Chain Home Low (CHL) and Chain Home Extra Low (CHEL) systems, until it was eventually replaced with the more advanced ROTOR and Linesman systems in the 1950s.

Edom took over several of the abandoned Chain Home stations, refitting them with seismographs and other sensing apparatuses, in the hope that vampire activity could be detected at long range. At the very least, they would provide early warning if Dracula or another similarly powerful entity moved towards England. This network was called Chain Home Deep (CHD or, later, CD).

In addition to its stations along the English coast, Edom established other listening posts in West Berlin, France, Switzerland, Romania, Gibraltar, and Cyprus. Chain Home was mostly decommissioned in the 1990s.

This Out." Some Edom field agents can get over clever, leaving a tin cup underneath a dripping outdoor faucet, for example.

A similar, more subtle, flash is the letters *SZ* written on or pointing to something: this serves to indicate a dead drop (*szohordok* in Edom slang) or something else worth noticing.

Old-school Edom **recognition phrases** include, from Isaiah 21:

"Watchman, what of the night?"

"The morning cometh"

"And also the night."

And from Deuteronomy 23:

"Non abominaberis ..."

"... quia frater tuus est."

The first translates to "Thou shalt not abhor [the Edomite]," the second to "for he is thy brother."

The Edom **distress signal**, which doubles as a generic "this isn't what it looks like" message, is the phrase "valley of salt," or just the word "salt" or even just toying with the salt shaker or dumping out the salt or putting salt in the coffee you serve a fellow agent. The origin is a verse in the Psalms (variously Psalm 59 or 60 depending on the translation) referring to a defeat for the kingdom of Edom in the Dead Sea region.

The E Squadron **tactical hand signal** for "vampire" is the index and pinkie fingers open and pointing down while the thumb holds the other two fingers shut, like "throwing the horns" reversed. Used in SWAT, commando, or similar operations where silent communication is vital, it has also migrated to the field: an Edom agent may flash the vampire sign behind his back to warn a fellow watcher that a vampire is in view, for example.

SPECIAL EDOM MANEUVERS

These special maneuvers are available to Edom Agents. The Director may make them available to regular *Night's Black Agents* heroes at her discretion.

ACTIVE EVASION TACTICS

Prereq: Edom training, 1 point in one of the evasion abilities listed below

You train to hunt vampires, true — but you also train to realize when you are the hunted, and get out of there.

By spending 1 **Military Science, Architecture, Urban Survival**, or **Outdoor Survival** point (whichever is relevant to the battlespace — **Military Science** is always relevant) you identify the best possible exit route from a losing battle.

If you roll an unmodified 6 on a successful **Athletics** test to run away (*NBA*, p. 61), and your enemies chase you, they must make *two* successful Athletics tests on the first round in the ensuing full contest or lose you. If they continue the pursuit, your Lead begins at 7 in the thriller chase. You also get a 3-point Athletics refresh.

If you do not roll a 6, but still succeed on the running away test, you only receive the 3-point Athletics refresh.

Directors may modify the Difficulty of the escape test for supernatural foes, usually by +1 (+2 for Vampiric Speed).

FRIEND IN DEED

Prereq: Edom training; either Athletics 8+ or Military Science 1+

E Squadron ratings train to work together as teams to contain or terminate vampires and other threats.

Once per combat, if you make a Feint (*NBA*, p. 74) to help a teammate, or a Support Move (*NBA*, p. 76), you can refresh 3 points of the ability you spent to do so: Hand-to-Hand or Weapons for the Feint, Athletics for a Support Move. You must narrate the Feint or Support Move action.

If your team wins that fight, you can refresh 1 additional point.

RAT SAW NOTHING

Prereq: Edom training; Disguise 5+ or Surveillance 5+ with Vampirology

You train to specifically avoid vampiric surveillance. You might:
- take detours through fancy hotels, hospitals, or other places rats avoid
- check mirrors and reflections constantly in peripheral vision for people who don't show up in them
- notice flinches or other reactions near churches or holy ground
- notice brief hesitations while crossing sewer mains or door frames

- change up your smell regularly with cologne or spicy food
- stay under overhangs to thwart owls and bats

By narrating such a countermeasure, you receive a 3-point refresh of either Surveillance or Disguise. If it's really original or clever, the Director should give you a 4-point refresh and write it down as another standard Edom counter-vampire countermeasure.

At the Director's discretion, she might also lower the Difficulty of **Sense Trouble** tests when you enter an area you know to be potentially vampire compromised: cemeteries, rat-infested alleys, etc.

EDOM TACTICAL FACT-FINDING BENEFITS

The Director should encourage trained Edom Agents to act like it and work the TFFB system (*NBA*, p. 107) for all it's worth. Here are two special Edom TFFBs to get started with.

TARGETED ARSON

The Agents need to dose the likely combat area with accelerants, or conceal incendiary devices therein. **Architecture** can identify non-load-bearing or well-aired places to set fires, or **Military Science** can determine the likely ambush or battle site. With a Difficulty 4 **Explosive Devices** test (or a Difficulty 5 **Athletics** test to throw an incendiary) the Agents trigger the flaming ambush once their vampiric foe has entered the fire zone. The fire does its usual damage, and the tactical constraint and shock reduce the enemy's Aberrance or Hand-to-Hand pool by 6 until the fires go out (a number of rounds equal to the margin of success on the triggering test roll).

THE WATER METHOD

The chosen area must have running water: a river or brook, ideally. By mapping the site and timing the tides with **Urban Survival** or **Outdoor Survival** (whichever applies) the Agents can channel the pursuit of (or escape from) their foe. They receive a team pool of 3 points each in the relevant chase ability, which they can spend on Cooperation or assign to the lead pursuer or runner.

VAMPIRE SEASON

Whether due to the natural fluctuations of the earth's magnetic field while orbiting the sun, or to the vagaries of the liturgical calendar, there are some times when vampires are even more dangerous.

There is not an especially favorable season in which to hunt vampires, except as a general rule when daylight hours are longest, in June.

In the Balkan tradition of the Sabbatarian or *sâbotnik,* one born on Saturday, the Jewish Sabbath, hunts vampires more effectively. Edom personnel records show no particular correlation of combat effectiveness and birth day. Dogs born on Saturday, however, show a slightly higher ability to track the Un-Dead (reroll the first unmodified 1).

VAMPIRE NIGHTS

St. George's Eve (April 22 Gregorian, May 5 Julian): A night for witches and fire magic in the Balkans. Blue fires traditionally burn over buried treasure, or anywhere that unquiet blood or vampires lie.

Walpurgisnacht (April 30 Gregorian, May 13 Julian): In many pagan traditions, May 1 marked the closing of winter and the beginning of spring, a liminal time or "hinge of the year." The last night of winter, therefore, was particularly powerful for malevolent forces getting one last lick in. Its shifting nature makes it particularly propitious for witches, werewolves, and vampires. In the Julian calendar, this is also the last day of the ancient Roman festival of Lemuria (May 9–13), when the walking dead were propitiated and exorcised. Vampires in Italy may be more dangerous throughout May.

Halloween (October 31 Gregorian, November 13 Julian): The other traditional "hinge of the year," six months after Walpurgisnacht. Edom reports widely vary: in some places, Halloween is almost completely silent, while in others Un-Dead activity peaks as in Walpurgisnacht.

St. Andrew's Eve (November 29 Gregorian, December 12 Julian): Known as the "vampires' night" in Romania. During this night, dreams can turn prophetic, and animals speak. To speak to such beasts risks death — as does being outside at all, since vampires stalk the land in a frenzy.

EFFECTS

On St. George's Eve and St. Andrew's Eve, increase vampires' Aberrance by one-fourth, rounded up.

Vampires gain Regeneration at 1 point of Health per round per century of un-life (round up).

On Walpurgisnacht (and Halloween if the Director wishes), increase vampires' Aberrance by +1 per century of un-life (round up).

Werewolves and other shapeshifters (if they appear in the campaign) also increase in power on Walpurgisnacht; add +1 to Health for every 5 points in Aberrance (round up). They also regenerate +2 more Health per increment than normal.

Telluric energies are particularly unpredictable and dangerous on these nights (+2 to all Difficulties to operate earthquake machines, for example; pp. 40–41), and where vampires walk, blue balls of St. Elmo's fire follow. Harker's report indicates that some of those balls do indicate the location of buried treasure: a 2-point **Archaeology** spend allows a watching Agent to mark the place for later excavation. Assuming she survives the night, of course.

Necromancy (whether by vampiric power or something like the Spirit Board (*DH*, p. 279)) may be easier on All Souls' Day (November 2), when the dead (usually the worthy or virtuous dead) approach the living.

Edom places all its facilities on alert during these periods. On the off chance that the Orthodox calendar is the controlling calendar for vampiric power increases, Edom facilities go on alert on the Julian dates as well, which fall 13 days later.

HISTORY OF EDOM

The moment when the *Demeter* crashed with spectacular force upon the rain-drenched shore of Whitby, when an "immense dog" leapt from the bow of the wrecked ship to land upon the sands of England, was the culmination of decades of planning by a handful of dedicated and determined spymasters.

Dealing with the repercussions of that moment, those plans, would take far longer.

This is the "standard secret history" of Edom, known to Edom agents with **Tradecraft** 2+ or those who catch Oakes in a loquacious mood at the Ley Arms in Exeter. The Director may well have a "true secret history" buried deeper in the files, obtainable only by in-game investigation.

1876-1893

Armies clashed across the East during the Russo-Turkish War of 1876–1878, and the British military establishment watched with interest as their faltering and untrusted ally battled their old enemy. Among their agents numbered Dr. George Stoker, at the time a surgeon with the Red Crescent, and scholar Armin Vambery. Both these men were considered reliable and trustworthy informants, so when both

EDOM: 1730?

The earliest reference to vampires in English comes from the pamphlet *The Travels of Three English Gentlemen*, published originally in 1734, and describes a grand tour of Germany and Eastern Europe undertaken by the nameless trio.

The anonymous author of the pamphlet was likely the Reverend John Swinton, who visited Slovakia and the surrounding regions in 1734, only a few years before the catastrophic earthquake of 1738 that shook the Vrancea region of Romania. Swinton transcribes a paragraph from Professor Zopfius of the University of Essen:

The Vampyres, which come out of the graves in the night-time, rush upon people sleeping in their beds, suck out all their blood, and destroy them. They attack men, women and children, sparing neither age nor sex. The people attacked by them complain of suffocation, and a great interception of spirits; after which, they soon expire. Some of them, being asked, at the point of death, what is the matter with them, say they suffer in the manner just related from people lately dead, or rather the spectres of those people; upon which, their bodies, from the description given of them, by the sick person, being dug out of the graves, appear in all parts, as the nostrils, cheeks, breast and mouth &c turgid and full of blood. Their countenances are fresh and ruddy; and their nails, as well as hair, very much grown. And, though they have been much longer dead than many other bodies, which are perfectly putrified, not the least mark of corruption is visible on them. Those who are destroyed by them, after their death, become Vampyres; so that, to prevent so spreading an evil, it is found requisite to drive a stake through the dead body, from whence, on this occasion, the blood flows as if the person was alive. Sometimes the body is dug out of the grave, and burnt to ashes; upon which all disturbances cease.

---

reported strange, almost supernatural encounters, in the Carpathian Mountains, their superiors were bound to take them seriously.

The first inklings of what would become Operation Edom consisted of modest investigation into the "vampyre" phenomenon, bringing the light of modern science to bear on peasant superstition. The man who would later operate under the nom de guerre of Peter Hawkins (**DH**, p. 39) put the problem to some of the best scientific minds in London. The members of the X Club (**DH**, p. 184) could be relied upon to mount a genuine scientific study without succumbing to religious dread. Their initial examination of Vambery's reports and the existing folklore suggested that there was a drop of truth within the myth. They also uncovered hints that the Catholic Church and other governments might also be aware of these creatures.

Hawkins decided that this was a weapon worth pursuing. Initially, this project was a personal obsession, without the sanction of the British government, but after Hawkins gained his leverage within (or control over) the new Naval Intelligence Division in 1887, he was able to bring the necessary financial and organizational strength to bear on the problem. He recruited more informants and agents in Romania, as well as a small number of confidants and experts in England who could be trusted to deal with the supernatural.

Hawkins and his agents conceived a plan, Operation Edom, with the goal of bringing a vampire to England. This vampire Count would be lured with the promise of fresh hunting grounds in London. Suitable "victims" would be trailed across the Count's path. Once one of them became a controllable vampire, the dangerous foreign vampire would be imprisoned or destroyed, and the English vampire could then be studied in safe, controlled conditions.

1893-1894: DRACULA

At what point did the Dracula plan go wrong? Was it when Dracula devoured the *Demeter*'s crew and caused the ship to crash instead of landing safely at Whitby? Was it when Seward called in Van Helsing? Or when Kate Reed uncovered the existence of Dracula's circle of followers? Everyone who was involved in the case — those directly involved, like Seward or Harker, and those in the shadows, like Hawkins and his agents — had reasons to conceal the extent of their dealing with the Un-Dead.

The Count retreated back to his fortress in Transylvania, pursued by Van Helsing and the other hunters. Quincey Morris and Jonathan Harker inflicted apparently lethal injuries to Dracula, putting an end to the Count's menace for the present.

1895-1917: A THING OF SHADOWS

In the aftermath of the Dracula case, the Naval Intelligence Division reorganized its supernatural section. Hawkins — or his successor — was given a black budget to hire expert advisers, codenamed after the biblical Dukes of Edom. Edom spent the next two decades going back over "the old ground which was, and is, to us so full

EDOM'S VAMPIRE?

At some point in its history, Edom acquired a vampire. The most likely explanation is that it captured one of Dracula's victims in 1894 — perhaps the accounts of Lucy's death in the Dracula Dossier are fraudulent, or maybe it secured the elusive Juliette Parton or some unnamed third victim. Another possibility is that Mina Harker was not freed from the Count's cursed baptism of blood, and became a vampire when she eventually died, many years later.

More outré candidates also present themselves: Kate Reed might have been unable to recall the full extent of her torments on that terrible Friday the 13th at Coldfall House, and she too might have been tainted by the Un-Dead. Dracula might have turned one or more of his Satanic cult, or perhaps Edom was able to secure a Bride (Van Helsing's account of how he slew all three sleeping vampires notwithstanding).

Alternatively, maybe Edom found its vampire later on. The Dukes might have found some weaker vampire in Transylvania in the 1920s, or abducted a newly raised vampire in the chaos of 1940. Edom's vampire might not even have been a vampire at all — perhaps it offered sanctuary to Alraune (**DH**, p. 62) or experimented with even stranger derivatives of the Seward Serum.

Edom almost definitely had a vampire or some supernatural entity under its control in the 1980s and 1990s — or it acted very much like it did, as a disinformation op against its foes in Romania, Russia, or MI5.

Does Edom still control a vampire? Has it had more than one over the years, unable to keep the monsters alive? Does it destroy its vampires whenever the creatures show signs of growing too strong?

of vivid and terrible memories."

It obsessively correlated and re-examined the accounts of the principals as well as all the preparatory research conducted by the X Club and by the NID fact-finding expeditions to the Balkans. It went further afield, dispatching archaeologists and explorers into the Middle East on the trail of Lilith, digging up tombs and the graves of suicides in Transylvania, and tracking down every rumor of the supernatural from Greenland to Hong Kong.

It went over the meager consolation prizes of the original operation — a few samples of blood; some evidence recovered from the Count's safe houses; the remains of certain victims; Aytown's photographs, sketches, and paintings; and relics recovered from Dracula's domain. It began the earliest experiments with the Seward Serum, although that research would not bear fruit for many years.

Fear of contagion held Edom back at every turn — the one definite conclusion that could be drawn from the original operation was that they had been devilishly lucky. Dracula could have created a much larger circle of vampires to prey on the teeming millions of London. There might have been hundreds, then thousands, of vampires, instead of the handful that Edom knew about. Vampire lore suggested that such outbreaks were not uncommon in the past, and that it was only through prompt action by local hunters coupled with relatively small and isolated rural communities that contained the vampiric curse. Turn-of-the-century England did not have an established folk tradition for dealing with vampires, and the railway meant that London was only a few hours from any part of the country. One misstep could unleash disaster; Edom's work with what was effectively a biological weapon informed the development of the Royal Engineers Experimental Station at Porton Down in 1916. Edom satellite bases were established in remote locations, where they could conduct experiments and research in relative safety.

The original band of hunters as well as those others who came into contact with Dracula during his time in England were monitored. Some were permitted to sink back into relative obscurity, although Edom continued to watch them and their families. Others were approached for recruitment, on the grounds that staunch men and women who had already faced down Dracula once before were certainly Edom material. Others it watched and did not approach, suspicious of their true motivations and associations. Others it watched and approached only once; indulgences were granted to deal with those who could not be relied upon to stay silent.

And, of course, it put into place safeguards to ensure Edom would stay buried. The publication of *Dracula* in 1897 was just part of the cover-up. Carfax, for example, was literally buried — the house was razed and a new street built over it within a decade of Dracula's departure.

After twenty years, though, Edom was still no closer to accomplishing its original aim of securing a vampire as an agent. No proposed second attempt was deemed likely enough to be worth the risk of contagion.

1917-1940: PRESERVING THE EMPIRE

Edom came under the umbrella of the Secret Service Bureau in 1909. As tensions rose with Germany and Russia, Edom's lack of forward progress made it harder and harder to justify allocating resources to the operation's original goal. Edom's full-time staff dwindled to a handful of caretakers and a few aging analysts, although serum research continued under the auspices of the Admiralty's Experimental Department. Dukedoms went unfilled or assigned to part-timers.

Edom survived as an active operation thanks to the patronage of Winston Churchill. The future prime minister learned of the existence of Operation Edom in the early 1900s through London Freemasonry (or possibly through other means), and discovered its particulars when he met with Bram Stoker in 1908. When Churchill became First Sea Lord in 1911, he took a particular interest in Edom's potential, and secretly advocated for a return to Castle Dracula throughout his career.

It was during this period that Edom's few remaining analysts began to suspect the existence of one or more parallel vampire programs. Edom still had an excellent network of informants and watchers in Romania, the Balkans, and parts of the Middle East, as well as a few agents scattered in unlikely places around the globe, but was blind to events in world capitals. Its watchers might record German archaeologists digging up Dacian ruins, or suspicious orders to Bucharest Communist groups coming straight from Moscow, but without better assets in Berlin or Moscow, Edom could only speculate about its counterparts.

1940-1941: EDOM PHASE II

Churchill reactivated Edom on 9 April 1940. The initial operational brief was the same as in 1894 — to secure the services of a powerful vampire for the British Empire. Edom proposed a joint mission with the Special Operations Executive, but events overtook their preparations. The loss of much of northeastern Romania to the newly formed Moldavian Soviet Socialist Republic heightened Churchill's fears that the Soviets had their own vampire program and had entered into the Molotov-Ribbentrop Pact in order to buy time to recruit their own vampiric assets.

On 30 August, Germany transferred northern Transylvania to its Hungarian allies: possible cover for a Nazi vampire program? Edom hastily assembled, trained, and briefed a scratch commando team. The plan: parachute into Romania, contact (or, if necessary, awaken) Count Dracula, and offer him Allied support and recognition if he took over as much of Romania as he wished and held it against any foreign invaders or domestic entities.

The mission failed. Edom's team parachuted into Romania on 2 November 1940. On the 10th a huge earthquake struck the country, heralding Dracula's awakening. For some reason, however, Dracula rejected the Allied offer and chose to bide his time instead. The Edom team found itself caught up in a coup attempt by the occult-minded fascists of the Iron Guard in January 1941, and the Nazis swept into Romania, crushing the Iron Guard but bringing the oil fields of Ploiești under Axis control.

1941-1951: EDOM AT WAR

This second failure would have devastating repercussions for Edom in the future, but in wartime there was little appetite for recrimination. While the mission to Romania had not achieved its primary goal of turning Dracula against the Axis, the reports from the survivors strongly implied that the Nazis had their own supernatural warfare operation. Long-standing fears that Van Helsing should not have been trusted were re-awakened. Edom survived by positioning itself as the United Kingdom's defense against occult weapons. "D" conjured up images of an England overrun by Nazi vampires, hinting that the Reich's push into Romania was motivated less by oil and more by other concerns.

Edom established links with MI5, interrogating suspected German spies and potential Renfields. Deputy Head of "Five" Jasper Harker's B Division took the

lead in the ultimately fruitless search for Nazi vampires or mind-controlled double agents. Edom briefed the members of Operation Autonomous before they parachuted into Romania on 22 December 1943, telling them the clues that might signal the presence of Dracula (including, ironically, the thick fog and unexpected winds that blew the parachutists into the hands of the Romanian security forces). There were Edom men with Ian Fleming's 30 Assault when it stormed through Germany capturing archives, and with MI6's Operation Surgeon snapping up Nazi scientists and industrial secrets.

And there were Edom men whispering in Churchill's ear at Yalta, advising him that giving the Soviets unfettered influence in Romania would be a disaster. Churchill reserved "10% USA/UK influence" in Romania in his negotiations with Stalin, and had in mind a very particular 10% centered on the Borgo Pass.

1945-1956: HUNTING MONSTERS

After the war, Edom fought to retain its identity as other factions within the clandestine services tried to tear it apart in petty squabbles. Without Churchill's secret patronage, enemies tried to steal Edom's treasures — MI6's Romania section coveted Edom's networks there, and the Royal Naval Scientific Service continued to horn in on serum research. Meanwhile, Five either wanted to take part of Edom for itself, or else cut Six out of the counterintelligence picture entirely by declaring that vampires weren't a threat to be taken seriously.

While their superiors fought and argued in Whitehall, Edom officers on the ground and behind the Curtain hunted vampires and former Nazis alike. The 1956 Suez Crisis was the last gasp of Edom's second un-life — after its director's proposal to use magic to overthrow Nasser was rejected in favor of a military invasion, and with Romania solidly in the Soviet sphere of influence, Edom was told to begin winding up operations.

1956-1977: EDOM IN SHADOW

Again, in the eyes of officialdom, Edom

dwindled down to a few key personnel, a few barely operational facilities, and a small research staff. This time, however, "D" and his Dukes were prepared for the withdrawal of official sanction. Allies within MI6 sheltered Edom, assigning secret missions to Edom-veteran officers, hiding Edom activity, and diverting money from the Single Intelligence Account to fund the secret operation. Edom had its own sources, of wealth and of intelligence, drawn from Hapsburg gold and contacts made as far back as Vambery's day. While Edom officially slumbered, half forgotten, the operation continued in an unofficial capacity, protecting the United Kingdom from vampires and other supernatural threats while trying to unlock their secrets.

The research wing finally began to produce useful results. Work with the new science of DNA sequencing uncovered a bacteriological connection to vampires, and the Blacknest monitoring station was turned to hunt for telluric traces of the Un-Dead as well as Soviet bomb tests.

1977-1978: THE MOLE HUNT

Even before Edom was officially reactivated to hunt for the mysterious mole, the operation was intimately involved with the case. Edom's network of informants and spies in Romania discovered that there was a highly placed mole in British intelligence, passing secrets back to the Securitate and then onto Moscow Central. After MI5 tried and failed to find the mole, MI6 took a long-delayed revenge for old insults dating back to the 1950s, and suggested that Edom be reactivated to investigate a supernatural connection.

The mole hunt was almost a Pyrrhic victory for Edom. It found the mole — Nicholas Loman, a translator of Romanian family — and plugged the leak, but in the process, it uncovered a vast web of corruption in England, and lost virtually all of its networks in Romania. The events of 1978 transformed Operation Edom once again. The Dukes were reshuffled, and a new generation of Edom officers took up the cup.

The rejuvenated Edom, re-designated the Section for Research Operations, was given official standing within SIS.

1978-1990: NEW BLOOD

Even while dealing with the remnants of Dracula's stay-behind network, and trying to rebuild its Romanian network with the assistance of the CIA, Edom was drawn into the infamous Irish problem. The Troubles in Northern Ireland had flared up again with the splintering of the Irish Republican Army into the Official and Provisional IRA as well as the Irish National Liberation Army (INLA). The new, more aggressive response by the British included the sanctioning of the use of methods rejected by previous governments.

During the 1980s and 1990s, one of the most important British assets was a spy within the Provisional IRA, a spy so highly placed that it's said the police were told not to act on any information that might lead to his arrest, or even that elements of the British Army were complicit in the killings. This crown jewel was known by a codename — STAKEKNIFE.

The name was a private joke by Edom, referring to their use of a vampire to intimidate and suborn enemies of the state. Throughout the 1980s, Edom ran a vampire under the cover of the Force Research Unit in Lisburn. Techniques developed in this domestic operation would inform the operation's later efforts against jihadi extremists.

1990-2007: RETURN TO ROMANIA

While Edom continued to have a declining role in domestic counter-terrorism, the fall of the Ceausescu regime, collapse of the Soviet Union, and subsequent opening of Romania to the West gave Edom the opportunity to return to Transylvania in force. They re-established contact with their remaining szohordoks and investigated the extent of Dracula's Conspiracy in Romania.

Seismic evidence suggested that Dracula — or another powerful vampire — had recently returned. Major earthquakes shook the Carpathians in 1986, signaling the creature's awakening, and again in 1990, implying it had returned to sleep, just as earthquakes in 1893 and 1894 bookended Dracula's period of strenuous activity during the original Operation Edom. Without their Master's guiding will, Dracula's own servants and networks were ripe for takeover. Convinced they had a free hand, at least in the short term, Edom raced to rebuild its networks in the country ahead of their rivals. By the centennial of the original operation, Edom was once again fully established in the land beyond the forest.

2007-NOW: PROJECT MONTSEIR

Though 9/11 triggered the War on Terror, it was the 2005 attacks on London on 7/7 that alerted the British government to the threat posed by home-grown terrorism. The battlespace had changed — radicalized youths in London could communicate with and be influenced by terrorist leaders and trainers across the world. Like trade and communication, terrorism had become globalized. The same threat existed both within British society and in distant countries.

As it had in 1977, Edom offered an answer. Properly deployed, a vampire could hunt down and destroy terrorists both at home and abroad. Deniable, unstoppable, infinitely effective. Once again, Edom officers entered Romania and made contact with servants of Count Dracula.

The century-old fulfillment of Peter Hawkins' dream came in the form of Project Montseir. Drawing on the work of generations of MI6 analysts, scientists, and spies, Edom was able to convince — or compel — Dracula and his kindred into the service of the United Kingdom and its allies, shepherding them to put their monstrous abilities to work in the War on Terror.

That's where you come in. Terrorists still threaten Britain. It's up to you to unleash Edom's own terrors on them.

SECTION THREE: DIRECTOR'S BRIEFING

> *Therefore hear the counsel of the LORD, that he hath taken against Edom; and his purposes, that he hath purposed against the inhabitants of Teman: Surely the least of the flock shall draw them out: surely he shall make their habitations desolate with them. The earth is moved at the noise of their fall, at the cry the noise thereof was heard in the Red sea. Behold, he shall come up and fly as the eagle, and spread his wings over Bozrah: and at that day shall the heart of the mighty men of Edom be as the heart of a woman in her pangs.*
>
> — Jeremiah 49:20–22, a prophecy of the destruction of Edom

NIGHT'S BLACK AGENTS – EDOM FIELD MANUAL

BUILDING EDOM

Certain facts are true in every **Dracula Dossier** campaign. Edom is a long-running operation by British intelligence (initially, the Naval Intelligence Division; later, MI6) to recruit and control vampires. Edom attempted to bring Dracula to England in 1894, tried to use him against the Axis in 1940, and discovered that agents connected to the Count were at large in England and Romania in 1977. Edom is run by a mysterious director, codenamed "D," and his council of special agents called Dukes.

Everything else is negotiable.

Just as a vampiric Conspiracy where Dracula just wants to brood and murder Turks from the redoubt of his secret Castle will deliver a very different campaign to one in which Dracula's got a century-spanning scheme to take over the world, your take on Edom will play a large part in how the campaign unfolds. Over the course of your players' investigation into the Dossier, you and they will discover the answers to questions like:

HOW BIG IS OPERATION EDOM?

To give some real-world perspective — MI6 has around 3,000 employees, the CIA around 20,000. Of course, for every actual spy, you've got 5 or 10 support staff, so an Edom of 200 souls might only have a dozen or so officers who can go toe to toe with a player character. Also, for every actual spy, there are dozens of informants and agents — the Securitate under Ceausescu had around 10,000 spies, but had half a million informants on its books.

◉ A **Dust**-mode minimalist Edom might consist of "D," "Dr. Drawes," and a few staff at Edom's HQ and labs, the 11 Dukes of Edom, and a few blooded field operatives and/or HMS *Proserpine* ratings. Say 30 or 40 people on the inside, all told. There's a somewhat larger pool of SBS veterans, MI5/6 officers, and other friendlies regularly called in to serve on shell squads, or that are assigned to monitor some field of interest to the operation. This larger group is not initiated into the existence of vampires, although some have seen enough to suspect. In addition, Edom has a large network of agents, informants, watchers, and special assets in Romania and England that can be activated as needed. The conspiracy is large enough to threaten the Agents, but it's still small enough that everyone who's actually part of Operation Edom could fit around the smaller banqueting table at Ring without having to squeeze.

A small take on Edom implies that it needs only a single headquarters, and that either Ring or the Exeter house is no longer in use. The campaign will involve a lot more exploring abandoned, derelict, perhaps haunted Edom facilities than active conspiracy bases.

◉ Edom's actual size is hard to judge in the **Mirror** mode. Other than "D," some of the Dukes, and a handful of security staff, everyone else is officially part of some other agency or department. Hound might be an MI5 officer, "Dr. Drawes" works for the NHS or Porton Down (the UK's biological weapons laboratory). Ian and Nails are active criminals by day, secret spies by night. Officially, even within SIS, Edom doesn't exist. Is it so top secret that not even other spies suspect its existence, or is Edom an off-the-books operation, a conspiracy within British intelligence? Maybe Edom was shut down years ago, but has continued on in secret? Anyone could be a secret member of Operation Edom, the ghost within the British intelligence-gathering machine.

Edom facilities like Exeter or Ring are likely in private hands, run by Edom through a shell company or owned by a secret conspiracy member. Operational headquarters might be hidden underground at Carfax, or on HMS *Proserpine*.

🔥 A **Burn**-mode Edom combines the above two approaches. Edom exists as a discrete entity within MI6 — it's an official but top-secret operation — but there's also a shadow Edom, a conspiracy of loyalists and sympathizers who aren't part of MI6, but know about the vampire project and its potential value, and who help shield it from official oversight and investigation.

🎯 Edom's aspirations and reach are global, and so it has a staff to match. It's still small and secret, but still has manned stations and listening posts all over the world. The Dukes each have a number of field officers reporting to them. **Stakes**-heavy Edom might be more heavily invested in weird technology or occult powers,

with earthquake machines or vampire blood serums as standard equipment.

If your player characters are agents of Edom at the start of the campaign, then give Edom some high-minded goals — protecting Western civilization, killing Dracula, stopping the rogue German vampire program — so that the players can feel like the good guys, and later turn on Edom for failing to live up to its true purpose. If you're using Edom exclusively as villains, then tie its evil schemes to the Agents' Drives — if someone takes Patriotism, then Edom's actively trying to use vampires to take over the British government. If someone has Programming, then it's Edom hypnotic conditioning or the after-effects of Seward Serum experiments.

WHAT'S EDOM'S STANDING IN MI6?

Operation Edom is a very long-running operation, predating the Secret Intelligence Service. Did the Service accrete around it, making it the un-beating heart of MI6? Has all of British policy in the last century

been determined, or at least influenced, by the secret knowledge of vampires? Or is Edom a foreign body that's been grafted on, an unwelcome leech that sucks money and assets from the host without giving anything back? Or is Edom an obscure, half-forgotten relic clattering away in some attic that sometimes throws up unexpected results? If Edom's a rogue or completely off-the-books operation, then it has no official standing, and works through blackmail, back doors, secret favors, and threats.

How important is the vampire program? Is Edom making a genuine, vital impact in the War on Terror, or is it just picking off low-value targets to justify its continuing funding? Does the CIA know about Edom, or is it just handing a list of names over to the British on the assumption that the "Section for Research Operations" is a codename for the Special Reconnaissance Regiment, the British counterterror and surveillance unit?

IS EDOM COMPROMISED?

Dracula almost certainly has some agents within Edom, despite all its precautions, but how high does the rot go? Is the mole from 1977 still in place — or has the mole retired or died (or "died") after leaving behind a new nest of Dracula's minions? Are some or all of the Dukes working for the Conspiracy? Can Edom be saved, or is the operation irrevocably tainted?

Even if Edom isn't run by Dracula, then how committed is it to using vampires? Are there still some who'd prefer to be hunting the Un-Dead, or is the whole operation committed to using the powers of darkness for the furtherance of British interests?

DOES EDOM HAVE A VAMPIRE?

Edom may have captured a vampire in 1894 (Lucy, if the accounts of her death were faked by Seward, or another vampiric child of Dracula), or later. They could have grabbed Mina Harker later in life, as her redemption at the end of the novel was predicated on Dracula actually being destroyed. They might have found some other vampiric entity over the years, or even had one or more of their own turned during the debacles in 1940 or 1977.

DIRECTOR'S BRIEFING ■ BUILDING EDOM

EDOM WITHOUT THE DOSSIER

If you're going for a Dracula-free game and using **The Dracula Dossier** as source material and inspiration for your own campaign instead, then Edom still works as a secret clued-in organization in its own right. It could be the former (or even current) employer of some of the Agents, or a sinister third party that gets between the vampire hunters and their monstrous targets (exactly the role it takes in **The Zalozhniy Quartet**, for example; see **The Edom Files**, pp. 177 - 179).

A Dracula-free Edom may still be involved in the War on Terror, or might be content keeping England free of vampiric horrors.

(It's also possible that Edom *had* one or more vampires, but subsequently lost them. Perhaps they escaped, leading to the establishment of HMS *Proserpine* as a secure holding facility. Or, maybe vampires don't thrive in captivity, or Edom was unable or unwilling to provide sufficient victims to keep them alive. Perhaps there's a Sealed Coffin (***DH***, p 278) or three stashed on the Rig or in some other crypt.)

If Edom has its own vampire, are they using this asset to carry out its assassination program, or does it keep its own vampire in reserve and outsource the actual killing to Dracula or his servants? Or are both sets of vampires, foreign and domestic, put to work striking at enemies of the state?

How does the actual assassination program work? Document 2200 (p. 12) implies that the vampires are shipped to the vicinity of the target, then set loose. Where are they shipped *from*, though? Are they carefully loaded into sealed coffins at HMS *Proserpine*, or does an Edom team collect them from some crumbling castle? It's possible that Document 2200 is a lie written for consumption by Edom's masters in MI6, and doesn't actually describe how the operations really run — maybe Edom's "Special Biological Asset Containers" are just decoys, or are crammed full of sacrificial victims, and the vampires make their own way to the target. Are the vampires ever really under control?

WHAT'S EDOM'S DEAL WITH DRACULA?

Is Edom running the Count himself as an asset? If so, why is he working for it? Or, perhaps more accurately, why does it *think* he's working for it?

A threat so simple that even a medieval warlord can understand it, perhaps: "We know how to kill you. You thought four men with knives and Winchesters were bad — we can have twenty SBS hard men with UV projectors and silver-jacketed sniper rounds at your Castle by dawn. Work for us — or else."

Edom might have supernatural leverage of some sort — maybe it found a weapon that can slay the Count, or has a line on the source of his power, or just finally tracked down that translation of the *Zohar* or the right Orthodox rite to burn Dracula with a crucifix?

A bribe? Edom might have something Dracula wants (and needs for his capstone plot), or a prisoner to trade in exchange for his service. An incarcerated Bride, maybe — or just the names of a few Legacies, so Dracula can take his long-delayed revenge!

Alternatively, Edom may believe that Dracula is dead, sleeping, or otherwise sidelined, and have instead cut a deal with his minions. Or maybe Count Dracula himself doesn't participate in person (except when he wants to stretch his fangs), but he graciously allows Edom to borrow his servants and children/Brides as needed.

In any case, think about how Edom's communicating with the Conspiracy. Are there go-betweens working in the shadows of London and Bucharest? Does Edom have to send a messenger into the Carpathians, some latter-day Jonathan Harker carrying a list of targets, or do they just meet Dracula by the dockside in Galatz before ferrying him off to his next job? Is Dracula languishing in a sealed coffin in an Edom vault or moping in the ruins of his Castle, or does he sit in on the monthly departmental conference call?

FUTURE-PROOFING THE DOSSIER

Historical games are, ironically, timeless. Stoker's genteel late-Victorian horror, the all-too-real horrors of the Second World War, and the paranoia of the 1970s are all fixed. Their tropes are defined, their events recorded. Present-day games are another matter — the post-2011 section of **The Dracula Dossier** is a snapshot of the time it was written, and will inevitably be overtaken by events. This book, for example, was written in September of 2015, but you might be reading it five or ten years in the future. Here are some ways to keep the material relevant.

THE MARCH OF TIME

In 2011, when "Hopkins" obtained the Dossier, a soldier who was 22 years old when WWII began would have been 88. Although having a few nonagenarians running (or hobbling) around isn't that suspicious (especially in a campaign that's all about immortal monsters), look to replace most of the 1940s and many of the 1977 NPCs with their younger successors. Instead of interviewing the Balkans Specialist, the Agents meet her students. The Pensioner's long since gone, but her neighbor knows something useful.

For that matter, if there's an especially big gap between "Hopkins" discovering the Dossier in 2011 and the Agents getting their hands on it, you may wish to tweak her own backstory. Did she hide it again

AFTER THE WAR ON TERROR

The human villains of the campaign aren't especially relevant to the overall story. Al-Qaeda's on the decline already, overtaken by even more radical jihadists, so you can pull AQIR out and replace it with some other terrorist group (Edom previously used vampires against Republican terrorists in Northern Ireland; if some other bogeyman has seized the headlines, then use them instead). Send Dracula after ISIS, or after human traffickers, or after the Russian FSB if relations between East and West continue to decline. The villains are a device to justify the use of vampires.

for years before the Agents discovered it? Has she been on the run for years instead of the default days or months? (Alternatively, tie the return of the Dossier to some more recent earth tremor in Romania.)

Fortunately — from an adventure-writing perspective, if nothing else — the world isn't going to run out of conflicts anytime soon.

EUROPEAN POLITICS

Edom's old-school approach to espionage shields it from the vicissitudes of European politics. It predates the European Union, and won't be changed significantly if the United Kingdom breaks up, or leaves Europe, or both. An upheaval or crisis in Romania might have a bigger effect on the campaign, especially if it's on the scale of the upheaval in the Crimea that overtook the opening adventure of **The Zalozhniy Quartet**. If such an event occurs, then the best thing to do is read all the NPC and node write-ups as descriptions of their state before things changed.

PEOPLE OF EDOM

In a normal **Dracula Dossier** campaign, Edom is an elusive, sinister force, and the Agents must discern the shape of the threat by questioning the many NPC contacts, experts, and witnesses. The burned spies in a normal campaign will spend much more time in the company of retired SOE commandoes, Bucharest street cops, or eccentric occult experts than they will in direct contact with any actual members of Edom.

All that gets flipped around in a *Fields of Edom* campaign (p. 103). Here, the Dukes aren't mysterious rival agents glimpsed through the fog (or, in the later stages of a game, a sniper scope) — they're the player characters' co-workers, bosses, or even friends. A *Fields of Edom* game has lots of Edom internal politics and intrigue, so it needs more detail on those on the inside of the operation.

These NPCs follow almost the same format as those in the *Director's Handbook*, with some structural changes described below. In general, these NPCs aren't as multi-variant as those in the *Handbook*. Burned spies freewheeling across Europe in search of Dracula need flexible NPCs that can show up almost anywhere. The entrenched conspirators of a *Fields of Edom* game need a solid supporting cast to fill Edom's secret bases and overseas stations. Instead of using the Innocent/Asset/Minion triad of possible interpretations, these NPCs are broken down as being Stalwart, Unreliable, or Treacherous. (After all, they're all Edom assets).

Stalwart characters are pretty much who they say they are. They're loyal and reliable — for spies.

Unreliable characters have some dark secret, hidden agenda, or other compromising factor. They're not necessarily working against Edom, but they've got some ulterior motive or complication that makes them dangerous or troublesome to the player characters.

Treacherous characters are working against Edom. Usually, that means they've been compromised by Dracula's Conspiracy or some rival espionage organization.

DUKES OF EDOM

The 11 Dukes are Edom's senior operatives and supervisors. Each of them rules a Dukedom, a portfolio of agents, assets, and responsibilities within Edom. "D" is a distant, unseen presence; in most situations, the Dukes speak for Operation Edom.

ELVIS (DUKE ALVAH)

Role: Field operations in Eastern Europe and the Balkans

Description: Dark hair, dark suit, dark glasses — the demeanor of a car salesman, but the sort who'd sell you a high-end German car, not a used junker

Stalwart: Elvis has left the building — to run Edom's complex web of agents and szohordoks in Romania. The Alvah Dukedom is seen as a poisoned chalice; lots of influence, lots of power, but you're on the line for everything that happens east of Berlin. Even before the Night of Fangs in 1978, when the Securitate purged most of Edom's assets in Romania, being Alvah was a perilous and onerous duty.

The current Alvah, Elvis, handles his section with charm and calm. He's more in tune with the new Romania than the old — no longer haunted by superstition and the Communist past, but looking towards the

European Union and the high-tech future. Elvis' most commonly used cover is that of a trade attaché to the British embassy in Bucharest — that job alone keeps him very busy.

If one were to criticize Elvis, one might complain about his refusal to delegate. He has made himself dangerously indispensable. He runs his own networks and his own agents, and keeps all the relevant files in his head or on his own laptop. He compartmentalizes, so that no one else has the full picture of Edom's operations in Romania.

Elvis' hyper-focus on his own Dukedom means he's cut off from the intrigues of Edom politics in the United Kingdom. **Negotiation** and the promise of assistance when he's in the UK can buy help from him abroad. He's also cut off from Project Montseir, even though most of the terrorists targeted by it are in or have connections to Romania.

Unreliable: As above, but Elvis is too entangled in Romanian politics to be wholly trustworthy. Everything, even orders from "D" himself, gets weighed in his complex network of favors, obligations, debts, and grudges. He'll stall an Edom operation to benefit some Romanian ally of his, or trade favors in ways that don't necessarily benefit Edom. To Elvis, his Edom duties are an annoying distraction from empire-building in the shadows of the Romanian government. **Bureaucracy** or **High Society** gives the Agents enough sway for Elvis to take notice of them and make a deal; **Streetwise** clues them in on the existence of potential blackmail material related to Elvis' more questionable decisions.

Traitorous: Elvis' obfuscation of Edom operations in Romania is deliberate — he's hiding the real nature of his information sources. He might be relying on contacts within the CIA or SRI instead of cultivating his own independent networks, which means that the CIA or SRI knows everything that Edom does the Balkans. **Traffic Analysis** or **Tradecraft** digs up evidence that Elvis is too close to another agency.

The other, more alarming option is that Elvis has been compromised by Dracula. The Count's influence runs deep in that country, and when Elvis tried to rebuild Edom's networks, most of the agents he recruited were already the Count's servants. Is Elvis an honest fool, still loyal to Edom but deceived by the agents he's supposed to be running, or has he too entered into the service of Dracula? The Count's too canny to risk hypnotizing or using other supernatural coercion on a Duke, so **Vampirology** won't work — the Agents will have to use old-fashioned **Tradecraft** and **Bullshit Detector** to spot the sources of bad intel coming out of Romania.

Alternate Descriptions: (1) mid-30s, Oxbridge educated, runs everything she can remotely or on a spreadsheet, relies on subordinates for actual legwork [new broom parachuted in, so to speak, to sort out problems in Romania section]

(2) late 60s, always telling war stories, convinced the Russians are the real danger, runs up an impressive bar tab when meeting Agents [Old Edom veteran put back into harness]

(3) mid-50s, either a native Romanian or a perfect accent, cover identity of mining engineer, operates under the radar of Romanian government [former Securitate butcher given asylum in England]

Defining Quirks: (1) knows the manager by name in every good hotel in Romania; (2) different girlfriend every week; (3) speaks a dozen languages fluently, eager to practice on native speakers

Investigative Abilities: Criminology, High Society, Human Terrain, Languages, Streetwise, Tradecraft, Vampirology

General Abilities: Athletics 8, Disguise 12, Driving 4, Hand-to-Hand 8, Health 10, Infiltration 5, Medic 4, Network 25, Shooting 8, Weapons 6

Hit Threshold: 4
Alertness Modifier: +2
Stealth Modifier: +1
Damage Modifier: −2 (fist, kick), +1 (9mm Glock 17 pistol)
Armor: −2 vs. bullets, −1 vs. other (police tactical vest)

FORT (DUKE MIBZAR)

Role: Explosives and special weapons

Description: Afro-Caribbean, square shoulders, muscular, close-cropped hair

Stalwart: From its foundation, Edom has taken those offered to it by fate. If a schoolmistress or an American adventurer or a madman can serve, then serve they shall. For every two spies or soldiers, the operation has recruited academics, defectors, self-proclaimed psychics, even criminals.

Even, perhaps, monsters.

And even victims, although that doesn't quite apply to Fort. A vampiric monster

(perhaps a Feral Child Vampire (**DH**, p. 191), some spawn of a renegade 1894 Vampire (**DH**, p. 53), or even a mutated Jack) attacked Fort's family home in Brixton when she was 14, killing her mother. When Edom officers investigated the incident, they discovered Fort standing over the monster's coffin, with a petrol bomb in one hand and a lighter in the other. Impressed by the young woman's fortitude, Kenaz arranged for her to be educated at a boarding school and trained at Edom's expense.

One degree in chemical engineering, a placement with 11 Explosive Ordnance Disposal Regiment, then through the Intelligence Officers New Entry Course (IONEC), and into the Dukedom that had long awaited her.

She's made it her life's work to hunt down and destroy vampires — more, to make them scared of her. To be a monster to the monsters, to burn away her own fears with enough thermite and C4. She barely tolerates any "tame" vampires used by Edom, if such things exist. To other Edom officers, she's either coldly dismissive or one of the lads, depending on whether or not you've seen action against the Un-Dead. **Tradecraft** and a combat record win her trust. Everyone else should go through Tinman.

Unreliable: Fort is terrified of vampires, and the only thing that reassures her is high explosive. She needs to be in control, and equates control with more firepower. As long as operations are proceeding smoothly and everything's secure, she's fine. She can deal with crises, too — she's at her best when things are exploding and immediate action is needed.

It's the waiting she can't stand. The creeping fear that He's out there, in the darkness, looking for a way in. When Fort is under siege, she starts making booby traps and snares, and testing her fellow officers for signs of weakness or subversion. The combination of paranoia and explosives is an exceedingly dangerous one. **Reassurance** from someone she respects can talk her down; otherwise, she might well blow up part of Edom to save the rest.

Traitorous: Dracula has patience. If he has to sacrifice a young vampire to establish his agent's bona fides, if he has to wait 15 years for her to rise to a Dukedom, so be it. He is immortal. He can wait. He planted Fort for Edom to find, knowing that it would take in the orphan he made and raise it as its own.

Fort is unaware that she's Dracula's agent. Her hypnotic conditioning was laid down when she was an infant, and is buried so deeply that Edom's psychologists and counterespionage experts could never find it. Dracula might relay his orders to her telepathically — she tasted his blood with her mother's milk — or through some agent who contacts her at sunset on certain auspicious days of the year.

There's no safe way for the Agents to disarm this bomb. If they confront Fort with the truth that she's been a pawn of the vampires she hates all her life, she's likely to blow herself up. Their best bet is to lure her to a safe place before the final confrontation.

Alternate Descriptions: (1) mid-50s, boyish enthusiasm, always has the latest gadgets [member of absurdly rich banking family who blows things up as a hobby]

(2) early 40s, ex–Special Forces, injured by an IED, prosthetic leg with concealed stake [vengeful and bitter]

(3) mid-30s, always wears a lab coat and goggles, oddly reminiscent of a mole [lab tech promoted according to Peter principle]

Defining Quirks: (1) speaks loudly (she's used to shouting over ear protection); (2) carries a lighter but doesn't smoke; (3) works best to very loud music

Investigative Abilities: Chemistry, Cop Talk, Geology, Military Science, Notice, Vampirology

General Abilities: Athletics 8, Conceal 8 (Perfect Holdout), Disguise 2, Driving 4, Explosive Devices 12, Hand-to-Hand 8, Health 10, Infiltration 2, Mechanics 5, Medic 4, Preparedness 8, Shooting 6, Weapons 6

Hit Threshold: 4
Alertness Modifier: +2
Stealth Modifier: +1
Damage Modifier: −2 (fist, kick), +0 (flamethrower; **NBA**, p. 104), +1 (9mm Glock 17 pistol)
Armor: −2 vs. bullets, −1 vs. other (police tactical vest)

HOUND (DUKE KENAZ)

Role: Field Operations (UK & Western Europe)

Description: Short, red hair, vulpine face, hard eyes

Stalwart: Hound is Edom's agent in charge on the ground. She tracks vampire activity across the UK and Europe and

commands field operations like vampire hunts or cover-ups. As the Western Hemisphere falls within her domain, she's also Edom's primary liaison with the Cousins and other intelligence agencies, so she's on point for Project Montseir. That operation also adds the Middle East to her portfolio, leapfrogging Elvis' area of influence. He handles operations from Berlin to the Black Sea — everything else is Hound's.

She's logged a lot of frequent flyer miles in the last decade.

Everyone knows that she's the heir apparent to take over for "D" when the old bat finally moves on; she's politically unassailable thanks to her relationship with the Americans. She runs operations with frightening efficiency, and she's even better at extracting results. She can turn a good lead into great intel, but she can also rewrite information that's in the public domain and make it sound like insightful, top-grade analysis.

She's used to dealing with outsiders who aren't initiated into the secret world of Edom; she never, ever mentions vampires. **Cop Talk** is the best way to work with her; keep it professional, scientific, sane. She dislikes any implication that vampires are truly supernatural; she prefers to think of them as mutants with bizarre but ultimately rational abilities, not damned revenants sent by the Devil.

Unreliable: Hound's staked her career on Montseir. She needs it to work. Collateral damage, sacrifices, even betrayals can be justified as long as the operation gets results. As long as Montseir continues to deliver intel and dead hostiles, then Hound's future working relationship with the CIA, with MI6, and with "D" is assured. If Montseir fails ...

Nonsense. This isn't 1894 or 1940. They've thought of everything this time. Montseir cannot fail, only be failed. If there are problems, she'll deal with them. If there's trouble, she'll shoot it if necessary.

Agents with **Bureaucracy** know how invested Hound is in the success of her project. Stay out of her way with **Flattery** or she'll flatten any dissenters. She'll defend Montseir to the bitter end.

Traitorous: Hound knows something that the rest of Edom doesn't — she'll never become the director. Maybe "D" is immortal and will never retire. Maybe there's some blot on her record that she can hide but not erase. Maybe "D" simply doesn't trust her. Whatever the reason, she's risen as high as she can in Edom. No matter how successful Montseir is, there's nowhere else for her to go within the SIS.

So, she's looking for an alternative exit. The CIA is the obvious candidate — she could slide into a desk in Langley very comfortably. If that doesn't work, she could sell out to the Russians or the Chinese and vanish with a new identity and enough money to make it all worthwhile. In exchange, she's planning on offering one of Edom's crown jewels (a vampire, perhaps, or an Earthquake Device (**DH**, p. 266), a literal jewel like the Westenra Brooch (**DH**, p. 284) or a Jeweled Dagger (**DH**, p. 270), or maybe even the Dracula Dossier itself).

Alternate Descriptions: (1) mid-50s, obese, always on the laptop, gourmand [modern-day Mycroft Holmes; runs his section from limos and Michelin-star restaurants]

(2) early 40s, close-shaved head, leather jacket, every third word a profanity [ex-cop]

(3) late 50s, thin and severe, dresses like a headmistress, witheringly sarcastic [long-term Edom officer; may be much older than she looks]

Defining Quirks: (1) the coffee is the life; (2) takes out her crucifix when she senses trouble; (3) visits her brother and his kids whenever she's in London

Investigative Abilities: Cop Talk, Criminology, Interrogation, Law, Military Science, Tradecraft, Traffic Analysis, Vampirology

General Abilities: [second set of ratings is for Mycroft Holmes–esque version of the character] Athletics 8/2, Disguise 2, Driving 4, Hand-to-Hand 8, Health 10, Infiltration 2, Medic 4, Network 0/20+, Shooting 8*/2, Surveillance 6, Weapons 8*/2

Hit Threshold: 4, 3 [if Mycroft Holmes–esque]

Alertness Modifier: +2*

Stealth Modifier: +1

Damage Modifier: –2 (fist, kick), flexible baton (+0), +2 (9mm Glock 17 pistol)

Armor: –2 vs. bullets, –1 vs. other (police tactical vest)

* She has Special Weapons Training with her Glock and her flexible baton. If the Agents haven't spent Conceal, Criminology, etc., to cover their tracks as appropriate, Hound finds their traces. When Hound is in the area, all Heat and surprise Difficulties for the Agents increase by 1.

DIRECTOR'S BRIEFING ■ DUKES OF EDOM

IAN (DUKE IRAM)

Role: Courier, wheel artist, and occasional assassin

Description: Shaved head, silver teeth, Russian prison tattoos

Stalwart: Some Dukedoms come with a portfolio. Alvah has always monitored the Balkans; Osprey is always Edom's lamplighter; Magdiel has always, in one form or another, eavesdropped and intercepted communications. Others are redefined in each generation.

Previous Irams have been messengers, watchers, archaeologists, linguists. Ian, the current Duke, was thrown out like shrapnel from the Ukrainian civil war, and picked up by Elvis first as an asset, and then as a full-fledged Edom operative. Unlike most of the other Dukes, he's not MI6 and operates without state sanction, although he does have a British passport.

Ian divides his time between the UK and Romania. In Romania, he's Elvis' field man, running agents and overseeing operations outside Bucharest. In the UK, Edom uses him for illegal jobs that its MI6 superiors wouldn't approve — surveillance, bugging, intimidation, even the occasional fatal traffic accident.

[SU] If vampires need to be invited into a home, then he sleeps in his car. It's up to the Director whether or not that has any effect, but Ian thinks it does.

Human Terrain or **Criminology** works out that Ian is personally and unshakably loyal to Elvis. He'll follow the older Duke into Hell or the Red Room, whichever comes first.

Unreliable: Ian's ex-Mafiya. Elvis helped smuggle him out of the Ukraine when some of Ian's former comrades wanted him dead. They still do — if certain elements of the Russian Mafiya knew where Ian was hiding, either he'd be dead or Edom would have a lot more bodies to clean up. Ian may be building up his own

criminal outfit with Edom resources (with or without Edom's blessing — he might frame it as building connections within the Romanian gangs, or just siphon off cash and Seward Serum for his own use).

A **Network** contact (or **Criminology** coupled with an **Intimidation** bluff) can pressure Ian by threatening to sell him out to his old friends.

Traitorous: Two options — if you're tying *The Dracula Dossier* to *The Zalozhniy Quartet*, then Ian's breach with the Russian Mafiya is a ruse. He's a member of the Lisky Bratva (optionally, he's the Driver; *ZQ*, p. 10), under orders to infiltrate Edom and steal its vampire secrets for Dr. Dorjiev. He might sabotage an SBA assassination, stuff the Edom vampire into the back of a high-powered car, and make a break for the Russian border (run *The Zalozhniy Sanction* in reverse, starting in Vienna and running to Odessa, if you take this option.)

The other option is that Ian's grudge against his former comrades compromises his judgment. Either he gets into lethal trouble in Russia and needs the Agents to extricate him, or he lies about criminal targets for Montseir and gets Edom into a tit-for-tat spy-killing blood feud with the Russian vampire program (***DH***, p. 76). **Bullshit Detector** gives a brief warning before Ian goes rogue.

Alternate Descriptions: (1) mid-40s, short and unassuming cockney accent, wears heavy silver rings on left hand [ex–MI5 officer who quit to study the occult; drove a black cab for some time before being recruited by Edom]

(2) early 30s, short hair that fits under a helmet, average build, favors bulky jackets [Commando Helicopter Force pilot; she's an avid flyer]

(3) mid-20s, muscular frame concealed by tailored suits, deceptively soft voice, cover as an investment banker [addicted to Seward Serum; if it's nighttime, he's got 12 unassigned points he can drop on any General ability other than Cover, Disguise, Mechanics, Medic, Network, or Shrink]

Defining Quirks: (1) if he smiles, run; (2) keeps key rings as trophies; (3) hates routine and deliberately breaks his patterns every so often

Investigative Abilities: Criminology, Intimidation, Languages, Occult Studies [ex–MI5 only], Outdoor Survival, Streetwise, Urban Survival

General Abilities: [second set of ratings is for pilot version of the character] Athletics 8, Disguise 2, Driving 16*/8, Explosive Devices 5, Hand-to-Hand 8, Health 10, Infiltration 2, Mechanics 10, Medic 4, Piloting 0/12, Shooting 6, Weapons 6

Hit Threshold: 4
Alertness Modifier: +2
Stealth Modifier: +1
Damage Modifier: −2 (fist, kick), +1 (9mm Glock 17 pistol)
Armor: −2 vs. bullets, −1 vs. other (police tactical vest)

* Ian has the equivalent of Special Weapons Training with cars (+1 to all damage to others from crashes),

and can make Critical Hits (double damage on a 6 if his roll + spend beats the target's Hit Threshold by 5+) with a car impact.

NAILS (DUKE JETHETH)

Role: Wet worker

Description: Pale, floppy hair, loose baggy clothes, looks younger than he is

Stalwart: Nails' family was part of the Loyalist paramilitaries, fighting an illegal war against Irish Republicanism. The Troubles ended before Nails could do anything more criminal than keeping watch while his father and uncles delivered punishment beatings. He tried to join the British Army, but ended up doing mercenary work in Africa and the Middle East for a few years. Home on leave, some old school friends of his revealed they were now in the drug-dealing game, and they were having some trouble with IRA competition. Would Nails do them a favor and drive their rivals out of Belfast?

Seventy-two hours later, a dapper young fellow entered Nails' jail cell and introduced himself as Osprey.

Edom needed what might be termed "freedom of violent action" — it needed its own in-house killer. The Dukedom of Jetheth was traditionally the seat of Edom's official vampire slayer, but in this brave new era of Special Biological Assets and Project Montseir, killing vampires was very much secondary to clearing a path for them. For his part, Nails was only too happy to serve Queen and Country by killing people. **Bullshit Detector** suggests that what you see in the sociopathic murderous bastard is what you get. Nails is a happy man who whistles as he works.

Unreliable: As above, only Nails is disturbingly fascinated with vampires. At first, it was professional jealously — why invest all these resources in a bunch of pale skinny fuckers when he could do the job with

DIRECTOR'S BRIEFING ■ DUKES OF EDOM

CAR GADGETS

Ian has access to custom car-related gadgets from the Edom garage. In addition to the ones listed below, he regularly uses an NOS injector (**DT**, p. 71) and magnetic number plates (**DT**, p. 71).

Bomb Car: When you've got time to pack the whole body of a car with explosives, you can set up a really big bang. Ian's bomb cars aren't your clumsy lump of plastic explosive stuck to the underbelly — they're works of art. It takes a close examination (Difficulty 6 **Conceal** or **Explosive Devices**, or Difficulty 8 **Sense Trouble**) to spot one of these vehicles. Standard operating procedure is to park the car outside a target, and then walk away before detonating it remotely; a nastier Edom with its own vampiric assets might make use of hypnotized suicide drivers.

Distraction Strobe: A handheld flashlight-sized device with hundreds of piercingly bright LEDs, designed to flash in a sequence that provokes nausea and distracts the victim. It works similarly to the dazzle laser (**NBA**, p. 102). The attacker must make a successful **Shooting** attack; on a hit, the victim needs to make either a **Health** or **Athletics** test (Difficulty 8; their choice of ability) to avoid being blinded for one round, and a Difficulty 6 **Driving** test to avoid an immediate crash. Ian's especially adept at using this gadget, and can use Driving instead of Shooting when making a drive-by stun attack.

Wired Car: This car is fitted with a suite of surveillance gear, concealed within the body of the car. It comes fitted with directional microphones, a cellphone tower spoofer that lets it intercept mobile communications, and a custom Bluetooth-hacking black box that enables it to remotely connect to the in-car microphones of any modern vehicle with a hands-free system and use them to eavesdrop on any conversations that take place within. As all this gadgetry's built into the car, it's relatively unobstrusive when on a stakeout. There's no need for Ian to fumble with parabolic microphones or laser mics — he just parks with the car pointing in the right direction, and turns on the stereo.

his sniper rifle just as quick? Now that he's seen what vampires can do, he's entranced by them. He loves watching them work, watching them kill; he treats after-action reports like pornography. **Vampirology** picks up on the incipient obsession.

If left to his own devices, then Nails lets the vampires slip the leash more and more, encouraging them to take more victims and inflict more carnage to satisfy his own desires.

Traitorous: As above, only this version of Nails has made the decision to cross over. He wants to be a vampire, and is actively looking for a safe way to get turned without being immediately hunted down and staked by his former colleagues. He might "volunteer" for a vampire-hunting operation, kill the rest of the team, and offer himself to the monster. He might try stealing a sample of vampire blood, or just overdosing on Seward Serum. He might sell Edom out to Dracula or another vampire program, or try to rescue Edom's vampire (possibly after planting a nail bomb in Ring or HMS *Proserpine* to slow down pursuit).

Alternate Descriptions: (1) huge, bearded, indeterminate age, broken English [Kazakh vampire hunter]

NIGHT'S BLACK AGENTS - EDOM FIELD MANUAL

(2) mid-50s, owlish glasses, balding, might be a deputy headmaster or a bank manager [would never get his hands dirty, oh no, but knows every mercenary and assassin in Europe]

(3) early 30s but dresses younger, bleached-blonde hair, wiry, magnetic personality [mental issues aggravated by regular use of Seward Serum; as long as her delusions and murderous impulses accord with Edom's objectives, Edom's not going to get in her way]

Defining Quirks: (1) hand-rolls cigarettes, always offers one to his victim if the opportunity arises; (2) loves dogs, and they love him; (3) carries a hammer and roofing nails to work, just in case

Investigative Abilities: Human Terrain, Military Science, Notice, Streetwise, Urban Survival, Vampirology

General Abilities: [second set of ratings is for "deputy headmaster" version of the character] Athletics 10, Disguise 2, Driving 4, Explosive Devices 4, Hand-to-Hand 8, Health 10, Infiltration 2, Medic 4, Network 0/20 (to hire assassins), Shooting 16*/6, Weapons 10*/6

Hit Threshold: 4
Alertness Modifier: +1
Stealth Modifier: +2
Damage Modifier: −2 (fist, kick), +0 (knife), +1 (9mm Glock 17 pistol), +2 (sniper rifle)
Armor: −2 vs. bullets, −1 vs. other (police tactical vest)
* He has Special Weapons Training in his .338 caliber Lapua Magnum Accuracy International AWM sniper rifle (+2 damage) and his Fairbairn-Sykes fighting knife (+0 damage).

OAKES (DUKE ELAH)

Role: Analyst and archivist

Description: early 60s, dresses like a history professor, bushy eyebrows, never looks people in the eye

Stalwart: The oldest of the current set of Dukes, Oakes is the only surviving veteran — other than "D" — of the 1977 mole hunt. He's the only one who remembers the old Edom, when it was just a few old spies reading over death notices in the Romanian local newspapers and listening for distant earthquakes. He can't bring himself to believe that it's possible to control vampires — and certainly never trusts them.

He worked with "Cushing" (*DH*, p. 92) and the other key players in the mole hunt; he might even have been an assistant to the Alleged Mole (*DH*, p. 89) if Nicholas Loman was indeed the Alvah of that era. He's amassed a huge file on the hunt and related matters, like the later career of the Psychic (*DH*, p. 96), the strange commissions made by the Sculptor's (*DH*, p. 100) mother, and the legacy of the Romanian Securitate (perhaps through the Bucharest Private Detective; *DH*, p. 107), although he's long since given up on trying to convince "D" to reopen the case. Loman was the mole; he has to accept this.

These days, he works with Hound on selecting targets for Montseir and with

Elvis on cleaning up the mess afterwards. Neither of the two younger Dukes has much respect for him. **Flattery** works on the old man's ego; just don't get him talking about 1977.

Unreliable: It's time for Oakes to retire. He's past the regular retirement age of 60, although Edom always has a … flexible … attitude to older staff. His mind is slipping, and he doesn't have the energy to keep up with his younger colleagues. He clings on because he feels he has unfinished business; he doesn't want to retire until he identifies the mole and solves his first and last case. Any Agents assigned to work with Oakes are likely being groomed to replace him.

Whenever an Agent makes a **Bureaucracy** test (p. 34) for the Unreliable version of Oakes, roll a die. On a 1, increase the Difficulty by +2 to reflect Oakes' forgetfulness.

Either **Intimidation** or **Reassurance** can manipulate this version of Oakes; threaten to report his failings or help cover them up.

Traitorous: Oakes was the mole all along. His obsessive hunt is an elaborate bluff; by establishing himself as Edom's last great mole hunter, he discredits anyone who gets too close to the truth. Alternatively, it could be a genuine attempt to find the traitor, but he's got a hypnotically implanted blind spot. Not only is he incapable of remembering that he's the mole, he can't make the deductive leap to implicate himself. Getting unrestricted **Research** access to Oakes' files might allow an Agent to finally work out that he has been chasing himself all these years. A traitorous Oakes is compelled to report to his true Master once every few months, perhaps through a Conspiracy courier or through some sort of psychic channel.

Alternate Descriptions: (1) indeterminate age, shaved head, walks and talks fast [thinks faster], mouth reminds

you of a shark [sets up situation task forces with frightening speed]

(2) mid-30s, understated clothes set off by blue latex document-handling gloves, pale skin set off by dark hair [archivist and expert in medieval Transylvania; plans to digitize and cross-reference all of Edom's archives]

(3) mid-50s, commanding presence, twinset and pearls (crucifix at the end of the pearls, of course), adept at using glacial silences to intimidate [MI6 troubleshooter sent to clear up problems]

Defining Quirks: (1) takes pills for his nerves, and his liver — and for everything, really; (2) crossword fanatic, tests people by asking them to fill in clues; (3) sighs more than he used to

Investigative Abilities: Criminology, Cryptography, History, Human Terrain, Occult Studies, Research, Tradecraft, Vampirology

General Abilities: Athletics 6, Conceal 6, Disguise 2, Driving 4, Hand-to-Hand 6, Health 10, Infiltration 2, Medic 4, Shooting 4, Surveillance 4, Weapons 4

Hit Threshold: 3

Alertness Modifier: +2
Stealth Modifier: +1
Damage Modifier: −2 (fist, kick),
  +1 (9mm Glock 17 pistol)
Armor: none

OSPREY (DUKE OHOLIBAMAH)

Role: Edom lamplighter and analyst

Description: smooth features — could be anywhere from mid-20s to remarkably well-preserved mid-50s, small and well-dressed, Etonian accent

Stalwart: More than anyone else, Osprey runs Edom. He's in charge of day-to-day operations, reporting directly to "D" himself. Everything goes through him. Hound is the only other Duke with anywhere close to Osprey's degree of influence — she's got better connections to the Cousins, but he's part of the Establishment, the old school tie network that really runs the government. His family has been part of Edom since the beginning (optionally, he might even be a Hawkins Legacy), and he has never lost sight of the original goal of the operation. Edom exists to secure a reliable vampire as a spy and assassin in order to secure the future of the British Empire.

He appreciates quiet professionalism. He usually manages to mask his distaste for Nails, Ian, and Prince, all of whom he would like to replace with more suitable officers if possible. Agents who impress Osprey may find him to be a powerful if demanding patron. **Tradecraft** (or **High Society** and the right background) is the best way to deal with him.

Unreliable: As above, but Osprey is much more highhanded and callous. Everyone is just another asset to him; he has no compunctions about sacrificing agents, even other Dukes, in order to further the glorious operation. The only person in Edom he has any real attachment to is Edom's vampire, if it has one. Only a vampire can understand the detached, inhuman mindset he must adopt to do his job. Only an immortal understands the burden of history.

"Unreliable" isn't the best description of this Osprey — he's never going to turn on Edom, or sell out. He just doesn't give a damn about you or anyone else. People come and go, but institutions endure. **Negotiation** keeps you in the game as long as you're more valuable to him alive than dead — or Un-Dead …

Traitorous: Osprey's in love with Edom's vampire (or, if Edom doesn't have a vampire, then he's entranced by some secret vampiric lover, like Elizabeth Báthory (**DH**, p. 65), or a vampiric Carmilla Rojas (**DH**, p. 46)). She's the only one who's ever understood him; she's the ideal of Edom made into cold, Un-Dead flesh. He'd do anything for her — apart from betray Edom, of course; he'd never do that; but a little flexibility, a little shall-we-say indiscretion isn't a real betrayal. This version of Osprey will tie himself in endless knots of self-delusion

or doublethink to convince himself that he's still serving Edom's best interests. **Bullshit Detector** picks up that he's lying to himself.

Alternatively — if any of the Dukes could bypass Edom's anti-vampire defenses, it's Osprey. He knows which buildings have powerful defenses; he knows where the crucifixes and garlic are stored, as well as the blind spots in the security cameras. Furthermore, he's got the self-control to avoid recoiling in horror from sunlight or mirrors. Osprey's lover could turn him into a full vampire, and he'd be able to show up for work the next day without anyone noticing.

Alternate Descriptions: (1) early 60s, disheveled and shabby, bristly white mustache, bright eyes [might be mistaken for a janitor; Smiley-esque old spider]

(2) late 50s, scarred face and missing left hand, matronly attitude towards junior staff [gave up body and soul for Edom]

(3) late 60s, military bearing but a bit wobbly after lunch, persnickety about receipts and expenses [Edom lifer; did horrible things behind the Curtain in his youth]

Defining Quirks: (1) throws people off balance with odd or intrusive questions or observations; (2) almost supernaturally quiet footsteps; (3) tests everyone's loyalty — with the knowledge and approval of "D," of course

Investigative Abilities: Electronic Surveillance, Human Terrain, Law, Notice, Vampirology

General Abilities: Athletics 12, Disguise 8, Driving 4, Hand-to-Hand 8, Health 10, Infiltration 2, Medic 4, Shooting 6, Surveillance 16, Weapons 6

Hit Threshold: 4
Alertness Modifier: +2*
Stealth Modifier: +2
Damage Modifier: -2 (fist, kick), +1 (9mm Glock 17 pistol)

Armor: -2 vs. bullets, -1 vs. other (police tactical vest)

* Once Osprey has spotted the Agents, all of their Heat test Difficulties increase by 1 after 24 hours in the same city.

PEARL (DUKE PINON)

Role: Black bagger, thief, agent-at-large

Description: North Indian, elegant, long fingers, seductive smile

Stalwart: Pearl plays at being a 21st-century Raffles, a gentleman thief, but he's from a solidly middle-class background. His father is an electrical engineer who emigrated from India in the 1970s. Pearl developed expensive tastes at university, and was part of a circle of friends from much wealthier backgrounds. He committed a few petty thefts to fund his increasingly lavish lifestyle. When his crimes got him into trouble, one of his professors — an MI6 talent spotter, possibly the Retired MI6 Computer Boffin (***DH***, p. 99) — offered to make the arrest go away if Pearl considered a career with the Service.

Pearl is Edom's black bagger when needed, breaking into secure locations

to plant bugs or steal items. He's adept at operating undercover, and can pass for Afghan or Middle Eastern (he's fluent in Arabic, Pashto, Turkish, and Persian, as well as French, Spanish, and Romanian). Hound also uses him as a liaison officer when working with agencies and groups in the Middle East. He collects (or "collects") art as a hobby.

As an inveterate (and secretly insecure) social climber, trade invitations and **High Society** contacts to Pearl for favors.

Unreliable: Pearl is a compulsive thief and liar. He's a very good thief and a very good liar, and hasn't been caught out yet by his colleagues in Edom, but sooner or later his dissimulations are going to get someone killed. He might exaggerate how good his intel is on a particular terrorist cell, or his influence in the Indian Research & Analysis Wing. Confront him with **Interrogation** and proof of his lies to pressure him.

Traitorous: For all his insecurities and flaws, Pearl is loyal to Edom. He'll only turn on them if he has no choice. In this scenario, someone's got to Pearl's family — maybe one of his sisters got stopped by the Department of Homeland Security when trying to fly home from New York, or perhaps his father's suddenly been hospitalized for mysterious and inexplicable blood loss. He's been warned that if he tries to alert Edom, his loved one will be tortured and killed in response, and the blood will be on his pretty hands. **Reassurance** convinces him to trust the Agents; if they fail to rescue the prisoner in time, though, a suicidal Pearl sells out to another bad guy and vanishes.

Alternate Descriptions: (1) mid-40s, Welsh, small and taciturn, perfectionist craftsman [MI6 black bagger and security systems expert]

(2) early 30s, North African features, graceful and proud, complains about English weather [Italian thief arrested and recruited by Edom; optionally, she might be Menena Chakroun, the "queen of thieves" from *The Zalozhniy Quartet*, page 82]

(3) mid-50s, casual suit with a blazer and a leather satchel, sprig of mountain ash flower in his lapel [doesn't actually acquire items himself; Fagin-esque master of thieves]

Defining Quirks: (1) charming flirt; (2) perfectly manicured hands; (3) talented sketch artist

Investigative Abilities: Accounting, Architecture, Art History, Electronic Surveillance, Flirting, Forgery, High Society, Languages, Streetwise, Urban Survival

General Abilities: Athletics 12, Disguise 2, Driving 4, Filch 12, Hand-to-Hand 8, Health 10, Infiltration 14, Medic 4, Shooting 6, Weapons 6

Hit Threshold: 4
Alertness Modifier: +2
Stealth Modifier: +3
Damage Modifier: −2 (fist, kick), +1 (9mm Glock 17 pistol)
Armor: −2 vs. bullets, −1 vs. other (police tactical vest)

PRINCE (DUKE MAGDIEL)

Role: Hacker and computer expert

Description: skin like melted candle wax over thin bones, sunburnt, sour face, unwashed stringy hair

Stalwart: Prince is ex–Israel Defense Forces, out of their elite ELINT group, Unit 2800. She suffers from fibromyalgia, a painful condition that she treated with increasingly powerful medication. Discharged from the IDF because of her addiction to prescription painkillers, she moved to London. Her work with the IDF was enough to put her on MI5's radar, and Osprey approached her soon after she arrived.

Prince has little contact with the other Dukes. She rarely leaves her basement flat

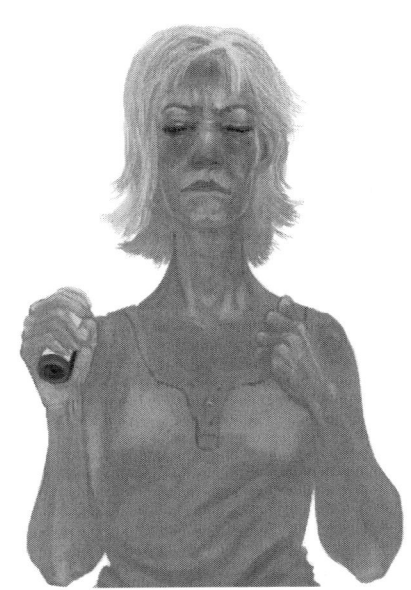

to attend meetings in person. She works through a stream of prickly, curt emails and the occasional brief untraceable VoIP chat, and is eternally frustrated and annoyed by the vagaries of the real world compared to the cold logical perfection of her realm. She keeps her constant agony from fibromyalgia a secret from her peers. Despite her complaints and seeming bad attitude, Prince is utterly committed to both Edom and its mission. She believes that Montseir is making a real difference in keeping both the UK and her homeland of Israel safe from Islamic terrorists, and is deeply grateful to Edom for giving her a chance to contribute. She respects professionalism; displaying good **Tradecraft** is the best way to work with her.

Unreliable: Part of Prince's bargain with Edom was that she would receive experimental treatments for her fibromyalgia. Regular injections of a dilute form of the Seward Serum give her the Unfeeling vampire power, blocking the pain from her condition. She rides each dose as long as she can, until she absolutely has to step outside or at least turn on a light other than the glow of her monitors. She can make one dose last for days, even weeks if she's lucky.

Know what happens to you when you spend virtually every minute of your life with vampire blood pumping through your veins? It's not healthy. It doesn't lend itself to stability. This version of Prince is a strung-out addict, careening between euphoria, paranoia, and depression depending on how long it's been since she had a hit. Feed her addiction with **Pharmacy** or undermine her with **Intimidation**.

Traitorous: Oh come on — the IDF just *happens* to drop an elite computer warfare specialist on Edom's doorstep, and it's coincidence? Please. Prince came to London under orders to let herself be recruited by the English vampire program. The only question is, does Edom know? Is this the start of a partnership between Edom and Sayeret Aluka, perhaps one orchestrated by Osprey? Or is Prince reporting back to her former employers in secret? (Or has her misuse of Seward Serum left her open to subversion by Dracula?) **Data Recovery** coupled with access to her computers turns up evidence of Prince's treachery.

Alternate Descriptions: (1) mid-20s, forgettable face, unruly hair, geeky T-shirt [on temporary loan from GCHQ; going to end up in a sports bag]

(2) mid-30s, freckled and ginger [humorless and utterly committed to Edom; researcher and analyst pushed into frontline role]

(3) mid-40s, greying and harried, chain smoker, [ELINT expertise a decade out of date; manages Edom's computer warfare section; was hoping to be promoted to Oholibamah but sidelined by the younger Osprey]

Defining Quirks: (1) moves awkwardly due to pain; (2) avid fan of vampire movies; (3) hates people intruding on her space

Investigative Abilities: Criminology, Cryptography, Data Recovery, Electronic Surveillance, Human Terrain, Pharmacy, Research, Tradecraft, Traffic Analysis

General Abilities: Athletics 4, Digital Intrusion 16*, Disguise 2, Driving 4, Hand-to-Hand 8, Health 10, Infiltration 2, Medic 4, Shooting 7, Weapons 4

Hit Threshold: 3
Alertness Modifier: +2
Stealth Modifier: +1
Damage Modifier: −2 (fist, kick), +1 (9mm Glock 17 pistol)
Armor: −2 vs. bullets, −1 vs. other (police tactical vest)

* Prince can call on dedicated resources from GCHQ for her hacking attacks, investigations, etc. This gives her a free full refresh of her pool every day.

TINMAN (DUKE TEMAN)

Role: Wire rat

Description: short and wiry, bad teeth (hit in the mouth by a rifle butt once), strong Glaswegian accent

Stalwart: Tinman's a former Royal Navy mechanic. He passed selection for the Special Boat Service and saw action behind enemy lines in Iraq, blowing up bridges and securing oil wells and pipelines. After leaving the Navy, he returned and spent six months volunteering with a charity, building houses and hospitals in the ruined cities. And after that, still searching for something to do with his life, he joined MI6 and ended up as Edom's engineer, building custom surveillance gear and anti-vampire weapons.

He has more direct experience of special forces operations and Arab culture than any of his peers in Edom, and is frustrated at being sidelined to a technical support role. He's convinced that if Montseir takes out the "right ragheads," it can bring about real change. His preferred hit list is six times longer than Edom's most ambitious threat matrix, and includes targets in the UK and USA.

He doesn't trust academics; the best way to get on his good side is to demonstrate genuine competence (**Tradecraft** or **Mechanics**) or to have seen action (have a genuine military background; **Military Science** or **Cop Talk** might let you pass as a former soldier).

Unreliable: Tinman's first loyalty is to his mates in E Squadron, not to Edom. He's sick of civilians risking the lives of good men for naught — it's all sexed-up dossiers and bad intel these days, and he hates having any part of it. Early in the campaign, he'll express his dissatisfaction in small ways; he might pass on extra equipment or information to E Squadron, or deliberately sabotage a mission that he feels is too risky so it never gets off the ground ("*Sorry we couldn't send an extraction team in to get you out of Sibiu, boss — the helicopter had engine trouble*"). Later, he might leak Edom information to the Journalist (**DH**, p. 120), or to some superior in the British government or intelligence services (the MI5 Deputy (**DH**, p. 95), perhaps, or the NATO Liaison (**DH**, p. 125)). And if that's still not enough, burn it all down. **Shrink** spots his increasing instability; **Mechanics** or **Notice** to spot evidence of his sabotage.

Traitorous: As above, but Tinman's acting under orders from somewhere within the Ministry of Defence. He's part of a plan to forcibly shut down and discredit Operation Edom, and put the English vampire project back under military control. Getting hold of a copy of the Dracula Dossier itself is one of his objectives; so too is digging up any of Edom's buried secrets that might be used to bring the operation to an end. If he finds any suggestion that Edom's been compromised by Dracula or some other foreign power, he'll follow that trail of clues to the end.

Alternate Descriptions: (1) late 50s, thinning hair, ascetically thin, high collars [Catholic priest who lost his faith; specialist in supernatural countermeasures]

(2) late 40s, looks like Thor gone to seed, smells of wood and welding, wears overalls [expert craftsman; makes beautiful stakes and sacred bullets according to age-old traditions]

(3) mid-50s, burly, wears a shawl, her strong Romanian accent incongruously peppered with London slang [ex-Romanian tank mechanic; expert in booby traps]

Defining Quirks: (1) just stopped smoking. Really. No more for him; (2) gestures with his baseball cap; (3) gets right in your face when arguing with you

Investigative Abilities: Chemistry, Electronic Surveillance, Human Terrain, Military Science, Notice, Occult Studies, Urban Survival

General Abilities: Athletics 8, Disguise 2, Driving 4, Explosive Devices 4, Hand-to-Hand 8, Health 10, Infiltration 2, Mechanics 10, Medic 4, Piloting 6, Shooting 6, Surveillance 6, Weapons 6

Hit Threshold: 4

Alertness Modifier: +2
Stealth Modifier: +1
Damage Modifier: −2 (fist, kick), +1 (9mm Glock 17 pistol)
Armor: −2 vs. bullets, −1 vs. other (police tactical vest)

TYLER (DUKE TIMNAH)

Role: Elegant muscle, political troubleshooting

Description: handsome, half-Chinese, athletic physique, Saville Row suits

Stalwart: Tyler's the son of a diplomat; his childhood was spent at embassies and international schools all around the world. He applied to join MI6 after leaving university, and was recruited by Edom as the new Timnah following the death of the previous incumbent in a car crash in Vienna. Like Pearl (whom he dislikes), he's sent as Edom's ambassador when they need to glad-hand some foreign politician or secret police chief. Through his family, Tyler is exceptionally well connected to the British government, especially the Foreign Office, so he's well placed to watch for political threats to Edom. Through his Masonic brethren, he has friends at the very highest level of the police service. Osprey especially relies on him to keep Edom free of entanglements or oversight.

High Society convinces Tyler you're the right sort of person and lets him relax and confide in you.

Unreliable: Tyler's running a disinformation operation targeting Room 452, the Chinese vampire program (*DH*, p. 75). He's posing as a greedy and ambitious Foreign Office bureaucrat with access to Edom's files, and is passing chickenfeed on to Room 452 via Hong Kong. The aim is to keep the Chinese away from Dracula and Romania, as the last thing Edom needs is more competition for that turf. **Tradecraft** alerts the Agents that Tyler might be giving the Chinese more than he

should, and **Data Recovery** finds traces of Chinese hacker intrusion into Edom's network. Has Tyler's plan backfired? Is Room 452 playing him instead?

Traitorous: Two options present themselves.

First, building on the Unreliable interpretation — Tyler might be betraying Edom to Room 452. His "disinformation" might be completely genuine intelligence, passed to the Chinese with the unwitting blessing and support of MI6. It would be trivially easy for Tyler to, say, send them a modern sample of the Seward Serum when he's supposed to be passing on an outdated formulation, or give them an out-of-date map on which he's secretly marked the correct location of Castle Dracula. **Traffic Analysis** could correlate Tyler's supposedly harmless leaks with Chinese activity in Romania.

The other possibility is that Tyler's a member of the Satanic Cult of Dracula (**DH**, p. 55). Several prominent Masons were part of Dracula's circle of worshippers in 1894; after the Count fled England, they continued to serve him from afar. There's been a secret lodge within the Grand Lodge for more than a century, and it is that Satanic cabal that holds Tyler's true loyalty. **Occult Studies** picks up rumors of a conspiracy within the secret society.

Alternate Descriptions: (1) early 50s, thin and sly, greasy hair, hooded eyes [blackmailer; digs up the dirt needed to protect Edom]

(2) mid-50s but aging elegantly, expensive tastes, adviser to certain senior politicians on security and international relations [former journalist, or SIS on very long journalistic cover]

(3) early 40s, stone-faced, blends into background, gravelly voice [makes problems go away]

Defining Quirks: (1) offers his hand in greeting (Masonic handgrip); (2) trains regularly; (3) dislikes being cornered

Investigative Abilities: Art History, Criminology, High Society [except stone-faced version], Human Terrain, Intimidation [stone-faced version only], Law, Negotiation

General Abilities: Athletics 15*, Disguise 2, Driving 4, Hand-to-Hand 15*, Health 10, Infiltration 2, Medic 4, Network 0, Shooting 6, Surveillance 0, Weapons 6

Hit Threshold: 4
Alertness Modifier: +2
Stealth Modifier: +1
Damage Modifier: −2 (fist, kick), +1 (9mm Glock 17 pistol)
Armor: −2 vs. bullets, −1 vs. other (police tactical vest)

* He targets the throat or wrists in Called Shots (**NBA**, p. 72) and Disarms (**NBA**, p. 73). Once per session, he can freely refresh 4 Hand-to-Hand pool points, as per Martial Arts (**NBA**, p. 75), or Athletics points, as per Parkour (**NBA**, p. 58).

SCIENTIFIC STAFF

Edom has fought to keep its medical research section in house, thwarting attempts by the British Navy and various Ministry of Defence groups to take control of the Seward Serum and other aspects of vampire research. The Blood is the Life, after all …

EARTHQUAKE TECHNICIAN

Name: Graeme Quicke

Role: Seismologist, demolitions expert, telluric expert

Description: early 40s, permanent thin-lipped scowl, cowlick, plastic raincoat smeared with many kinds of mud

Stalwart: Quicke's part of Fort's (p. 65) crew. He served with the Royal Engineers before being seconded to Operation Edom. (Optionally, he may have been recruited by the Seismologist (*DH*, p. 100).

If Edom has an Earthquake Device (pp. 40–42), then Quicke believes that manipulation of telluric currents is the real prize, and that vampires are just an epiphenomenon, a biological encrustation on a much more interesting geological phenomenon. Assisting with field operations or using the earthquake machine to topple buildings on top of troublemaking spies just takes time away from tracing the invisible map of subterranean currents.

If Edom doesn't have such a device, or if such devices don't exist in your campaign, then even the Stalwart version of Quicke is unhappy about his place in Edom. He wants to be sent to one of the stations in Romania, like NIEP (*DH*, p. 151) to continue his research. However, Fort keeps blocking his transfer requests; if the Agents use **Bureaucracy** or **Negotiation** to smooth things along, then they'll have an ally in Romania.

Unreliable: As above, but Quicke's even more abrasive. If he gets to play with an earthquake device, then he's a technical prima donna, expecting everyone else to accommodate him, and complaining about how complex and stressful his role is.

If he's just generally dissatisfied with his lot in Edom, then give him a drinking problem and make him pointlessly obstructive. (When in London, by the way, he drinks in the bar run by the Ex-IRA Informant; *DH*, p. 115 — which suggests he's looking for some sort of trouble.) He hates working for SIS, so he's decided to make everyone else miserable too. Fort has to tolerate Quicke's bad attitude because of his technical skills, so he's shielded from dismissal as long as he doesn't actually compromise a mission. Raise the Difficulty of all **Bureaucracy** tests by +1 if Quicke's around. **Intimidation** gets him to back off.

Traitorous: Quicke's experiments with telluric currents have brought him into psychic contact with some supernatural force. The obvious answer is that he's in thrall to Dracula, but he might also be under the influence of Zalmoxis (*DH*, p. 291) or Lilith (*DH*, p. 69), or maybe he's got some sort of weird connection to the cerneati (*DH*, p. 66). A really nasty version might be a take on Red Jack (*DH*, p. 73) where the serial killer spirit's managed to jump into an earthquake device, and is murdering whole cities instead of individual prostitutes (shades of the biblical tale of Sodom, perhaps?)

Alternatively, Quicke might have worked out the true location of the Scholomance (*DH*, p. 219) and taken a hiking holiday to Romania; is he now under the control of Dracula or the Solomonari (*DH*, p. 74 — or the Devil, for that matter?)

Shrink or **Vampirology** picks up

the signs that Quicke's under external influence — but possibly too late, if he's had ongoing access to an earthquake machine since he became compromised.

Alternate Names: Dominic Tate, Lucy Grey, Nicolas Ursu

Alternate Descriptions: (1) late 20s, went Eton to Oxbridge to Edom, long dark coat and scarf over Saville Row suit, manicured hands [architect and historian — just what you need when trying to resonate Castle Dracula]

(2) mid-30s, short but loud, overalls and hardhat, shouts to be heard over noise of machinery [civil engineer; expert in subterranean London]

(3) late 20s, pale with sunken eyes, movements remind you unavoidably of a lizard, heavy boots and gloves always [mountaineer and cave explorer; worked with NIEP]

Defining Quirks: (1) loves classical music, and pretends to conduct when generating quakes; (2) always asks before entering a room; (3) grumbles about work to anyone who's cleared to listen

Investigative Abilities: Architecture, Geology, Outdoor Survival
General Abilities: Explosive Devices 6, Mechanics 8
Alertness Modifier: +0
Stealth Modifier: +0

PATHOLOGIST

Name: Dr. Sarah Mason

Role: In-house physician and medical examiner

Description: early 40s; greying hair; wears a crucifix when on duty, but not otherwise; short-sighted

Stalwart: Dr. Mason is Edom's go-to forensic pathologist; her day job is at Charing Cross Hospital, a short walk from the SIS headquarters at Vauxhall Cross. Suspected vampire attacks get referred to her for autopsy (and cover-up, if needed);

the morgue at Charing Cross is equipped with a secret observation and containment room for corpses that might return to life, based off the designs for a similar chamber in the Munich Dead House (*DH*, p. 226). Dr. Mason thinks that vampires should be treated as a potential public health crisis — one vampire could be the vector for a mass infection if not properly contained. She's willing to believe that Edom is currently the best way to control the vampire threat, although if she learned about the SBA program / Project Montseir her faith might be shaken. Need a favor? Assuage her worries over an outbreak with professional **Cop Talk** or **Reassurance**.

Unreliable: Mason loathes "Dr. Drawes," and the two cannot work together. Edom needs both of them, at least until it can find a replacement for Mason (or she gets enough support at SIS to be appointed scientific adviser over Drawes). Her ambition coupled with her distaste for "Drawes" means she's started gathering evidence that could be used against the scientific adviser — reports on failed Steward Serum experiments, samples of serum and maybe even vampire blood, accounts of operations gone wrong because of the scientific adviser's overreach. If "Drawes" is involved in activities illegal under British law (like working with the Human Trafficker; *DH*, p. 118), then Mason's gathering evidence of this too. Plan A for her dossier is to use it to convince SIS that "Drawes" is a liability and should be replaced; Plan B is to leak it to the Journalist (*DH*, p. 120) or some figure in government (perhaps Lord Godalming; *DH*, p. 43). **Research** or **Notice** spots missing records; **Bullshit Detector** picks up on her dissatisfaction.

Traitorous: Convinced that Edom is one slipup away from a vampire plague update, Mason's taken it upon herself to organize an unofficial vampire-hunting cell. She has a friend in CO20, the Metropolitan Police's Territorial Support Group that handles riot control and containment; she may also have unofficially recruited other specialists and potential vampire hunters (in short, the sort of people who might be regular *Night's Black Agents* player characters). **Bullshit Detector** detects her nervousness; break into her emails with **Data Recovery** for proof that she's running her own unofficial Crew of Light on the side.

Alternate Names: Dr. Adi Sukarno, Dr. Malati Darzi, Dr. Alan Daubrey

Alternate Descriptions: (1) mid-30s, Indonesian, large dark eyes, black hair in a tight bun

(2) mid-50s, Indian, halting speech when not dealing with medical matters, uses a cane

(3) mid-30s, Old Etonian, puppyish glee at being a spy, noticeably fit and tanned

Defining Quirks: (1) treats religious items like scientific instruments — believes they have no inherent power, but can be useful as psychological weapons against superstitious vampires; (2) extremely well-organized, rehearses everything before she does it; (3) prone to depression, self-medicates to counter onset of black moods

Investigative Abilities:
Diagnosis, Forensic Pathology, Pharmacy, Vampirology

General Abilities: Conceal 4, Medic 8, Preparedness 4

Alertness Modifier: +0

Stealth Modifier: +1

PHLEBOTOMIST

Name: David Balogun

Role: Blood technician, vampire handler, interrogator

Description: early 30s, African, broad smile, wears open-collar shirts and latex gloves

Stalwart: Balogun is a nurse and medic recruited by Edom out of the NHS Haematology Research and Treatment Centre at Plaistow (*DH*, p. 195). He handles routine tasks — taking blood samples for testing, showing the proper procedure for using the various serums, maybe even taking blood packs (or live victims) to Edom's vampire, if it's got one. Nothing phases him; David's always warm and cheery even in the darkest of circumstances. People want to trust David; he's got the inside news from every part of Edom. His one weakness is **Gambling**; get him to relax over cards, and he'll share office gossip.

Unreliable: Balogun was "recruited" from Libya; he was a mercenary interrogator, working for Gaddafi's Mukhabarat. He was debriefed at a black site, and sold himself to Edom in exchange for a British passport and a commuted sentence. He's tortured and murdered people, but all his ghastly deeds have left no impression on his smiling face. Currently, he's on probation with Edom; he'll be moved to work with the interrogators on HMS *Proserpine*, or

assigned to work with the SBA program as soon as he's proved reliable.

Balogun's a survivor — if he learns about a better option, like jumping ship to the Russians or the Americans, or even the Conspiracy, he'll take it. Through some truly impressive double-thinking, he still nurses a grudge against Edom for their harsh treatment of him! **Tradecraft** or **Interrogation** notices telltale habits or picks up rumors about Balogun's past.

Traitorous: Balogun let himself be picked up by Edom; it got him where he needed to be. He's a secret member of a cult (perhaps worshipping Queen Tera (**DH**, p 71), or Lilith (**DH**, p. 69)), and Edom has sacred relics that rightfully belong to his brethren. His plan is to stay undercover until Edom's in crisis (if necessary, he can engineer a crisis, say by releasing a vampire or deliberately leaking information about an ongoing operation to some enemy agency), then grab the relics and flee back to North Africa. Go through his belongings with

Occult Studies to find some documents relating to his secret faith.

Alternate Names: Willie Reyes, Rosa Moss, Dr. Cynthia Reed

Alternate Descriptions: (1) mid-50s, crotchety old Navy sawbones, sarcastic, twinkling eyes [ex–Royal Navy medic]

(2) early 40s, unflappable, calls everyone "dearie," finds veins with unerring accuracy [former hospital matron]

(3) mid-20s, quiet, well-connected family, unnerving habit of taking your blood without you noticing [Reed Legacy]

Defining Quirks: (1) shakes everyone's hand firmly, as if testing their grip; (2) sniffs when taking blood, as if he likes the taste; (3) deep and hearty laugh

Investigative Abilities: Diagnosis, Vampirology [possibly Interrogation or Occult Studies for some variants]

General Abilities: Hand-to-Hand 6, Medic 6

Alertness Modifier: +1

Stealth Modifier: +0

SERUM RESEARCHER

Name: Dr. Ian Sykes

Role: "Igor" to "Dr. Drawes"

Description: late 20s, pristine lab coat over geeky T-shirt, bearded, expensive headphones permanently welded to ears

Stalwart: Dr. Sykes is part of the scientific adviser's research team, continuing to improve and refine the original Seward Serum formula. As the junior member of the research group, Sykes gets handed the jobs that "Drawes" doesn't want to do — interviewing and examining HMS *Proserpine* Jacks who've overdosed on the serum, cataloguing old blood samples at the Exeter archive or the Plaistow site, running long DNA analyses in the lab. Sykes was recruited as a graduate student out of Cambridge; he's used to this sort of academic overwork. **Shrink** tells that he idolizes "Drawes" as a genius; **Flattery**

coupled with the promise of putting in a good word with his boss gets Sykes' cooperation.

Unreliable: Sykes has his own variation on the formula that emphasizes the enhanced resilience (Health) granted by the Seward Serum. He intended it as an emergency medical treatment — stick a syringe into a severely wounded soldier to keep him alive long enough for conventional surgery — but has since discovered that a low-level dose of the formula coupled with a tincture of blood can keep tissue alive indefinitely. His lab (either at some Edom facility like Plaistow (**DH**, p. 195) or HMS *Proserpine* (**DH**, p. 169)) is a horror show of dissected-but-still-alive animals, disembodied limbs and organs, and literal brains-in-jars, all hooked up to a crazy network of pipes and tubes used to distribute the preservative formula. He's one Red Bull bender away from his own Frankenstein's Monster. This side project might be approved by "Drawes," or be Sykes' little secret (or, "Drawes" is using Sykes to carry out experiments that he knows Edom would not tolerate).

Get him talking with **Flattery** (or **Chemistry**) and he'll quickly let slip that he's working on something cool.

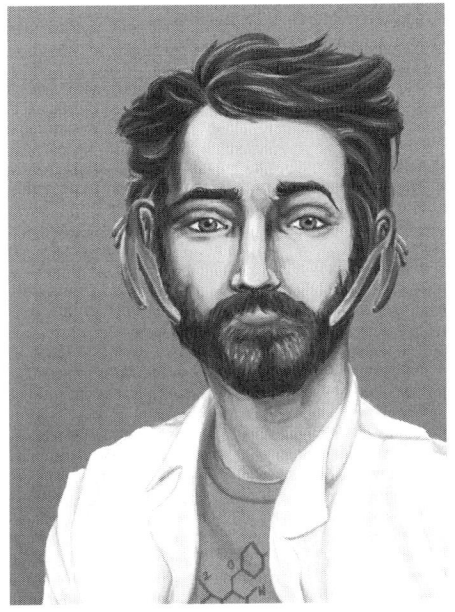

Traitorous: Sykes believes that the commercial applications of vampire blood are incalculably valuable — how much would the elite pay for immortality? Especially if that immortality comes with no vampiric drawbacks, no need to feed on blood or avoid sunlight or be damned for all eternity, just a regular injection. He knows he doesn't have the resources to develop this on his own — and that Edom would murder him if he tried. Therefore, his plan is to make contact with some international firm that might shelter him from Edom's wrath, and sell the formula to them. He might be in touch with the Pharmaceutical Researcher (**DH**, p. 128) or representatives from Nox Therapeutics (**DH**, p. 162) — or some larger company like Novartis or Sinopharm. **Accounting** detects suspicious payments into his account; if nervous, he tries to flee the country under a cover identity.

Optionally, this might be a play by some rival vampire program to get hold of Edom's stock of vampire blood.

Alternate Names: Dr. Chris Maunsell, Dr. Terry Scheffler, Dr. Adam Cula.

SYKES FORMULA

The Sykes formula gives 20 bonus Health points when injected, and the user automatically passes Consciousness rolls. The user doesn't die when reduced to −12 Health. Go below −20 Health, though, and you're dismembered (you still don't die, but you're not going to get better, either). The Sykes formula carries the same drawbacks as the Seward Serum (sunlight cancels its effects, addiction is a risk, obey the Master), and the two serums cannot be combined.

Optionally, Dr. Jacqueline Seward (**DH**, p. 47) can slot into this role.

Alternate Descriptions: (1) mid-30s, disconcertingly energetic, medieval weapons enthusiast [flagged for possible transfer to a field role]

(2) mid-50s, ex-military, stony-faced, haunted eyes [supervises testing of new serum variants on human "volunteers"]

(3) late 60s (maybe?), white hair and mustache, hunched shoulders, thick German accent [probably can't be a captured scientist from some WWII-era Nazi program, right?]

Defining Quirks: (1) drinks his coffee out of lab flasks; (2) perpetually sniffling; (3) condescending attitude towards non-academics

Investigative Abilities: Chemistry, Pharmacy, Vampirology
General Abilities: Digital Intrusion 4, Medic 4
Alertness Modifier: +0
Stealth Modifier: +0

HMS PROSERPINE RATINGS

E Squadron is the designation given to the Special Boat Service team assigned to HMS *Proserpine* and Operation Edom. The Special Boat Service has four other squadrons — C, X, Z, and M — as well as a Reserve squadron. The four active squadrons rotate through training, conventional operations, and counterterror operations, but E Squadron is permanently attached to Edom.

(If there's no HMS *Proserpine* rig in your game, then E Squadron might be headquartered at Carfax or the House in Exeter.)

SQUAD LEADER

Name: Captain Mark Sinclair
Role: Commander of one of E Squadron's troops
Description: early 40s, rugged, scarred lip, excellent physical condition

Stalwart: Captain Sinclair commands one of E Squadron's troops. He's absolutely dedicated to Edom and England; he signed up to fight for his country, and that's exactly what he's doing. It's not what he expected when he applied to join the special forces, but he long since came to terms with the existence of the supernatural. He has a healthy respect for vampires, just like he respects any dangerous weapon, but doesn't fear them — he's staked one or two in the past, and saw the expressions on their faces when they died. He's committed to Edom for life. **Bullshit Detector** tells you that he's not lying. A man like him doesn't need to. If he promises to get a job done, it'll get done. And if he promises that he's going to kill you, you're as good as dead.

Unreliable: Sinclair hates sloppiness. He wants defined mission parameters, hard targets, good intelligence. Over the last few years, he's clashed bitterly with all of Edom's Dukes, and fights any attempt to deploy E Squadron personnel without a full assessment of the dangers they might face. This inflexibility forces the player characters to rely on shell squads or their

own combat skills instead of calling in the special forces; a **Military Science** spend is required to get Sinclair to even listen to a proposal, and a bigger spend may be needed if the mission is especially murky or perilous.

Traitorous: Sinclair's career is stuck in a dead end. He's stranded on HMS *Proserpine*, outside the normal promotion ladder. He knows that Edom won't let him go, won't let him quit — so he's going to make them fire him, in a way that preserves both his life and the financial security of his family. He's writing a tell-all book about Operation Edom. He's in contact with a journalist (possibly the Journalist (***DH***, p. 120), the Tabloid Journalist (***DH***, p. 134), or the Dissident (***DH***, p. 112) — assuming the "journalist" isn't an undercover foreign agent) who's helping him finish the book. **Bureaucracy** notices his declining interest in doing a good job — he's already mentally checked out.

Alternate Names: Geoffrey Amstad, Angus McClin, Frank Gaskins

Alternate Descriptions: (1) late 40s, always looks tired, injured by IED in Iraq but refused medical discharge

(2) mid-40s, tall, impenetrable Scottish accent, fierce temper

(3) mid-40s, civilian clothes, heavy eyebrows, more like a Mafia hitman or enforcer than a soldier

Defining Quirks: (1) all stiff upper lip and understatement; (2) taps his pen on the desk when nervous or annoyed; (3) hates animals, especially dogs that look like wolves

Investigative Abilities:
History, Human Terrain, Military Science, Outdoor Survival

General Abilities: Athletics 10, Driving 6, Hand-to-Hand 6, Shooting 12, Weapons 10

Alertness Modifier: +2

Stealth Modifier: +1

VETERAN RATING

Name: Colin Fennell

Role: Staunch Edom soldier

Description: mid-30s, stocky, bearded, never idle

Stalwart: Fennell's the dependable bedrock of E Squadron. He keeps his head no matter what's going on, and is equally adept at undercover operations as he is at open warfare. Until recently, he had no ambitions beyond E Squadron, but he recently got married and has a second kid on the way, so he's started to think about moving to a civilian role if he can find one that's half as interesting and rewarding as protecting the United Kingdom from vampires and human monsters. He's agreed to stay on until Project Montseir is complete at least — he hates to leave a job half done. Secretly, he suspects that Edom will eventually have to go after Dracula again one day, and wants to be in on that kill team. **Bullshit Detector** picks up on his straightforward and trustworthy nature, but it takes **Reassurance** and proof that Dracula's completely out of Edom's control before he'll switch sides.

Unreliable: Fennell's a throwback to an older era of Edom — he's here to kill vampires, not babysit them. He hates the bloodsucking monsters. He'll follow orders and keep his loathing under wraps, but given the opportunity, he'd let a vamp burn in the sun or stake the monster himself rather than bringing it back for Edom to use. That said, he's an enthusiastic user of the Seward Serum, and is addicted to the strength and speed it brings. In his ideal world, they'd farm vampires for their blood, do unto the leeches what they used to do to us.

He also mistrusts civilians who get involved — anyone outside Edom could be a vampire thrall, so he assumes that renegade vampire hunters (like the average ***Night's Black Agents*** player

character) is a hypnotized mind-slave or Renfield for some unseen vampire master. He's extremely paranoid and occasionally violent when it comes to protecting his family and his privacy; his wife knows now that she must never invite anyone in. **Vampirology** or **Shrink** picks up on the extent of his hatred for vampires; leverage it with **Negotiation** or taunt him with **Intimidation** to get him to overextend himself.

Traitorous: Fennell's one or two Stability tests away from going completely rogue. He's going to vanish in the middle of some mission, and show up again six months later as a renegade vampire hunter and mercenary, selling his insider information on Edom to some rival vampire program; as long as they pay him (and shelter his family), he'll kill the dead for them. **Tradecraft** or **Outdoor Survival** notices that he's planning a departure — setting up supply caches, obtaining false travel documents, stockpiling ammo and cash, or making suspicious contacts. If confronted, he snaps and tries to fight his way out.

Alternatively, **Bullshit Detector** picks up that his loathing for vampires is just an act — he denies the Master in order to protect Him! Fennell might have already fed his family to Dracula, or else the Conspiracy got to him through them. His operating orders are to eliminate any Edom officers who might be a threat to Dracula's plans; if caught, Plan B is to free any captives on the Rig, then blow the self-destruct charges.

Alternate Names: Alan Duncan, Spencer Wright, Olivia Blake

Alternate Descriptions: (1) early 40s, scars on neck, slow and thoughtful [E Squadron "Chaplain"]

(2) late 20s, acne-scarred face, extremely fit, avid swimmer and climber [sniper]

(3) early 30s, unremarkable features, good at putting people at their ease [transferred from Special Reconnaissance Regiment; surveillance expert]

Defining Quirks: (1) slouches and sprawls when sitting; (2) eats unreasonable numbers of oranges; (3) cuts off any discussion of family or personal lives

Investigative Abilities:
Military Science, Notice, Outdoor Survival, Urban Survival

General Abilities: Athletics 12, Disguise 4, Driving 3, Hand-to-Hand 12, Shooting 12, Weapons 8

Alertness Modifier: +1

Stealth Modifier: +1

NEW BLOOD

Name: Mark Wyre

Role: New recruit

Description: mid-20s, dark-haired, piercing green eyes, pugnacious

Stalwart: Wyre just completed his special forces induction course with the SBS, having served for three years with the Royal Marines. As a new Special Boat Service member, he would ordinarily be assigned to one of the four active squadrons for a few years' tempering and experience before even being considered for E Squadron, but Edom has a special interest in Wyre — his mother is Romanian, from the mountains near the Borgo Pass. He speaks fluent Romanian, but otherwise knows nothing about the legends and beliefs of his mother's homeland. She hoped that her son's career would take him away from the shadows, instead of leading him even deeper into darkness.

Right now, though, Wyre's only read the Level 1000 documents, and believes that E Squadron is nothing more than a black-ops section. **Human Terrain** or **Languages** picks up on subtle oddities in his choice of words that indicate a Romanian background.

Unreliable: Wyre's mother, Lenuta, escaped Romania as a young girl in 1978, with the help of Edom — payment for help her family gave the operation during that terrible winter. Some senior Edom official (perhaps Elvis, p. 64, or Oakes, p. 34, or even "D," p. 25) has kept an eye on the Wyre family since then, visiting once or twice a year like an eccentric uncle. Wyre is utterly loyal to his mentor, so he may be used as a pawn in some internal power play. For example, if Elvis is running him, then he might arrange for Wyre to rise quickly though the ranks so Elvis can bring E Squadron under his control. **Research** or **Tradecraft** spots that someone tried to conceal Wyre's family connection to Edom in the records.

Traitorous: As above, but Wyre's mother is Ruvari Szgany; Dracula let her go, injecting her into Edom's collection of Romanian refugees and English szohordoks. The vampire is immortal and can afford to wait a generation for his plans to come to fruition. When in England, Wyre's mother made contact with other members of the Master's stay-behind network, and they helped train and prepare Wyre for his role. They helped

him shape his career, making him exactly the sort of person Edom likes to recruit.

His mission is to infiltrate E Squadron and report on its doings to Dracula. When the time comes, he will destroy it from within. He uses the Seward Serum to communicate with Dracula. Taking the serum puts him into a hypnotic trance in which he can speak to his Master, no matter how great the distance between them.

Diagnosis spots that he's suffering the aftereffects of the serum at unusual times; **Interrogation** cracks his carefully constructed surface personality and reveals the fanatic Renfield beneath.

Alternate Names: Bhagwanji Raja, Nick Fell, Marku Amache

Alternate Descriptions: (1) mid-20s, Mancunian, brilliant combat driver, hates cold weather

(2) mid-20s, confident, ambitiously already planning post-Edom career in politics

(3) mid-20s, family left Romania in 1980s, suffers from nightmares

Defining Quirks: (1) eager to prove his value; (2) unnervingly intense; (3)

keeps his mother's crucifix as a keepsake in his duffle bag

Investigative Abilities:
Military Science, Notice

General Abilities: Athletics 10, Disguise 2, Driving 3, Hand-to-Hand 8, Shooting 12, Weapons 4

Alertness Modifier: +1
Stealth Modifier: +1

SUPPORT STAFF

Edom's operation's administrative and secretarial staff generally know or suspect the truth, and have drunk from the cup, but aren't field officer material. Edom player characters deal with support staff every day of their working lives; those outside the operation will never knowingly meet them.

The majority of Edom's staff report to Oakes, Osprey, and Prince — or to "D" and his staff.

ARCHIVIST

Name: Henry Poole
Role: Edom librarian
Description: late 50s, tweed jacket straining to contain his belly, walks with a limp, laughs too much at his own bad jokes

Stalwart: Poole's part of Oakes' staff (based at the Exeter House, or Ring, or Carfax, or upstairs in the Asylum). He's one of the custodians of Edom's huge library of books, case files, documents, and maps relating to Transylvania and the Un-Dead. Poole considers himself something of an expert on the Dracula Dossier and the original 1894 and 1940 phases of the operation; anything after 1950 is beneath his notice as mere current affairs, not storied history. Even in his stalwart incarnation, he's an absolute prig, unwilling to cooperate without a **Bureaucracy** or **Flattery** spend. Few people ever visit his section of the archives, anyway, which suits

him perfectly well. Visitors only mess up his carefully organized files.

If the Agents bring him a new item for his collection (something like Renfield's Journal (*DH*, p. 277) or Van Helsing's bag (*DH*, p. 282)), he will answer any one question about the 1894 or 1940 operation that does not directly pertain to Dracula or vampires.

Unreliable: As above, but Poole's convinced that he and he alone knows the true secret of Dracula. He's obsessed with some obscure side trail — the role of Thornley Stoker, perhaps, or the Jeweled Dagger (*DH*, p. 270) — and is certain that investigating it will unlock the mysteries of the Un-Dead. Obviously *he* doesn't have the skills to do so, but you dashing young future Dukes, this is exactly the sort of thing you should be doing. He'll be Van Helsing to the Agents' Quincey Morrises as he gives them plenty of obscure leads to follow. Most of these will turn out to be time-consuming red herrings, but maybe one will pay off — and if it does, no force on Earth will be able to contain Poole's ego.

DIRECTOR'S BRIEFING ■ SUPPORT STAFF

If the Agents aren't willing to indulge his crankish beliefs, **Intimidation** forces him to actually do his job.

Traitorous: Poole's fallen into the orbit of some other occultist — pick from a connection to the sinister and entirely too-clever Psychic (**DH**, p. 96), an obsession with the Online Mystic (**DH**, p. 126), or even induction into the Satanic Cult of Dracula (**DH**, p. 55). His ally intends for Poole to steal some item from Edom's archives — and with Poole's skills as a forger, it might be months before Edom realizes it's missing. If Poole fears he's in danger of discovery, he'll present some new lead to the player characters, one that will send them into danger (*"Gentlemen! I've uncovered the true location of the fabled Scholomance! Off you pop!"*). **Bullshit Detector** picks up the bluff; **Interrogation** after the fact gets the truth out of him.

(Alternatively: Poole's the one who leaked the Dracula Dossier to "Hopkins." He planted the story about an automated monitoring program in a 40-year-old computer network to hide his own traces.)

Alternate Names: Tabitha Warren, Ross Tighlman, Jeremy Guinness

Alternate Descriptions: (1) late 40s, perpetual squint through thick spectacles, clothing in style 20 years ago

(2) early 40s but acts old (and pompous) for his age, tailored serge suit, tall and stiff-legged

(3) mid-50s, ginger hair going grey, beaky nose and blue eyes, short, wears horrible nylon jacket and rayon tie in all weathers

Defining Quirks: (1) holds papers up to his eyes to read them; (2) always bends neck downward in perpetual crouch; (3) thins lips when irritated and impatient, which is most of the time with outsiders

Investigative Abilities: Art History, History, Languages (Romanian), Research

General Abilities: Conceal 3
Alertness Modifier: −1
Stealth Modifier: +1 (soft walk of the librarian)

LOGISTICAL SUPPORT

Name: Courtney Barrow
Role: Support staff
Description: mid-30s, bleached-blonde hair, snub nose, Bluetooth headset

Stalwart: A vital cog in the Edom machine, Barrow handles the operation's transport and logistical accounts. She works out of MI6's headquarters at Vauxhall Cross. If you need an immediate flight to Tehran, or to ship a coffin from Cluj-Napoca to Cruden Bay, then she can arrange it all, quickly and efficiently. Her cheery voice on the telephone is a lifeline for stranded Edom agents in unfriendly lands. In the office, Barrow's full of chat but is careful to never give anything away through gossip. **Flirting** (or investing a **Network** point in her) is enough to get a quick look at her spreadsheets; couple that with **Cryptography** and **Traffic Analysis** to work out who's flying where on Edom's shilling. Barrow uses codes and numeric references for all travel requests, so she's not supposed to know who's where. She does, of course, but wouldn't admit that even to herself.

Unreliable: As above, but Barrow isn't quite so careful. Chatting to her with **Flirting** or **Flattery** gets her to reveal more information about Edom operations than she should — who's in favor with "D" and who's out, current targets, internal politics, and so on. She has no clue about the supernatural aspects of Edom; that Mr. de Ville is so annoying, with his insistence on only traveling by ship instead of taking a flight …

Human Terrain spots that Barrow is especially close to one of the Dukes; he or she has deliberately cultivated a friendship

with her in order to keep track of the movements of rivals.

Traitorous: Barrow's been turned by one of the other vampire programs using supernatural means. She might have a jenglot (***DH***, p. 67) squatting in her attic courtesy of Room 452 (***DH***, p. 75), or the Russians had the Retired KGB Agent (***DH***, p. 97) dig up a ghost to haunt her. Her performance in Edom has dropped precipitously since the supernatural invaded her life, but she knows that talking will only get her killed. **Diagnosis** spots that she's under stress, and **Reassurance** gets her to confess her treason. If the Agents don't take action, then their next overseas flight brings them right into the enemy's trap.

Alternate Names: Enid Jarrett, Adnan Khan, Julie Baird

Alternate Descriptions: (1) late 50s, big glasses, knitted cardigan, photo of her grandsons on her desk [office manager]

(2) mid-20s, cheap ill-fitting suit and tie, expensive backpack of computer parts [tech support]

(3) early 40s, graying brown hair, sweet tooth [inventory manager]

Defining Quirks: (1) calls all Agents "love"; (2) always has a pen, often toying with it in her fingers; (3) laughs at everyone's jokes, no matter how stale

Investigative Abilities:
Accounting, Traffic Analysis
General Abilities: Network 7
Alertness Modifier: +1
Stealth Modifier: −2

SECRETARY

Name: Mrs. Cretch
Role: Gatekeeper to "D"
Description: late 50s, maybe — sour expression, lined face, pursed lips — eyes like fire

Stalwart: Mrs. Cretch is the director's personal secretary and assistant. She is always by his side, traveling with him from his office at Vauxhall Cross to Ring. Everything goes through her — every phone call, every appointment, every operational detail. She is, it seems, the only person that "D" trusts implicitly. Office rumor insists that she's been around Edom since the beginning. The very beginning.

She's virtually impervious to any sort of manipulation — **Flattery** and **Intimidation** both fail to make a mark. Getting past her to see "D" without an appointment requires a **Bureaucracy** test (Difficulty 4 + 1 per player character, +1 per previous visit without an appointment).

Mrs. Cretch has buried better people than the player characters. She's seen countries fall. She's looked into the face of Dracula himself, and asked if he takes milk and sugar in his tea.

Unreliable: Mrs. Cretch is the director's last line of defense against supernatural threats. She might be a lamia (***NBA***, p. 151), or a bound jenglot (***DH***, p. 67) wearing a mask of leathery human skin. She might be an Alraune (***DH***, p.

62) cutting, resurrected through Edom weird science after the "real" Alraune reincarnated into a fresh mandragora, so Mrs. Cretch hates and resents her eternally young "sister." She might be an immortal Mina Harker or Kate Reed, kept alive with the Seward Serum. She might even be the 1894 Vampire (**DH**, p. 51).

In this setup, she's not so much unreliable as troublesome. A creature such as her must feed, and her murders must be kept discreet even from the rest of Edom. If the player characters are considered trustworthy by "D," then he may ask them to provide for Mrs. Cretch. If they're brave, they could even (**Negotiation**) use this insider knowledge as blackmail material.

Traitorous: As above, but all monsters ultimately pay homage to their Master. In her black and withered heart, Mrs. Cretch serves Dracula. She is the mole inside Edom, and has reported the director's every doing to the Count for more than a century. "D" is hopelessly reliant on her and cannot be convinced of her treachery — to admit that she's betrayed him would call everything he's ever done into question. Proof of her connection to Dracula coupled with **Negotiation** gets the Agents a 24-hour head start before he burns Ring to the ground with himself inside, or takes a walk down to the Thames with stones in his pockets. Whatever method he chooses, it'll be one that stops him rising in three days' time.

Alternate Names: Miss Hawkins, Mrs. Foyle, Mr. Twigg

Alternate Descriptions: (1) strangely ageless, blond hair combed perfectly, blank stare, ice-blue eyes

(2) 75 if she's a day, wizened face, apple cheeks, perpetual grandmotherly smile, dead eyes

(3) 40s or 50s, unlined face with deep tan, smooth jet-black hair parted combed straight back, thick black-rimmed tinted glasses

Defining Quirks: (1) never seen to eat, drink, or make tea; (2) rolls her r's when irritated; (3) sneaks looks at the letter opener on the desk, seems calmer afterward

Investigative Abilities: Seemingly any

General Abilities:

Network 20, at least

Alertness Modifier: +3

Stealth Modifier: +1

SZOHORDOKS

The Hungarian word actually refers to wooden benches outside houses and inns where one could sit and exchange gossip. In Edom parlance, it refers not just to dead drops but also to informants and assets. All of these szohordoks can be considered Edom assets, although few know anything about who they're working for or what's going on. They are all on the Edom rolls and their contact details are on file (requiring a Difficulty 3 or Difficulty 5 **Bureaucracy** test to requisition).

In addition to those listed below, the following characters from the *Director's*

Handbook could also be counted as szohordoks, at least in some of their incarnations. Characters listed in bold are especially sensitive and valuable assets (or politically embarrassing) if Edom's running them, and require a Difficulty 7 **Bureaucracy** test before their handler (Elvis, Hound, or Osprey, usually, or some local MI6 Asset Runner) makes them available for use.

Anti-Communist (*DH*, p. 81), Former Gehlen Org (*DH*, p. 82), **Neo-Nazi** (*DH*, p. 85), Pensioner (*DH*, p. 86), **"Van Sloan"** (*DH*, p. 87), Anthropologist (*DH*, p. 90), Balkans Specialist (*DH*, p. 91), Defector (*DH*, p. 93), **The Hungarian** (*DH*, p. 94), Psychic (*DH*, p. 96 — although he's probably got a big *DO NOT USE* stamp on his file), Seismologist (*DH*, p. 100), Art Forecaster (*DH*, p. 103), Bucharest Private Detective (*DH*, p. 107), **Bureaucrat** (*DH*, p. 109), **Chief of Station, Bucharest** (*DH*, p. 109), Chinese Agent (*DH*, p. 110), Drug Boss (*DH*, p. 113), Enigmatic Monsignor (*DH*, p. 114), Ex-IRA Informant (*DH*, p. 115), Human Rights Activist (*DH*, p. 118), Human Trafficker (*DH*, p. 118), Online Mystic (*DH*, p. 126), **Radical Imam** (*DH*, p. 129), Romanian Police Inspector (*DH*, p. 130; see also *Edom* entry for Romanian Mafia; *DH*, p. 158), Smuggler (*DH*, p. 131), **SRI Agent in Charge** (*DH*, p. 133), Tabloid Journalist (*DH*, p. 134). Any of the Legacies (*DH*, pp. 40–47) could also be in this category, especially **Philip Holmwood** (*DH*, p. 43) and Dr. Jacqueline Seward (*DH*, p. 47).

BUCHAREST NIGHT CLUB OWNER

Name: Sandu Ciocan

Role: Street-level contact and criminal informant

Description: late 40s, former gym rat going to seed, tracksuits by day — expensive suits by night, sweaty palms

Stalwart: Sandu runs Club Copacabana in Bucharest — not the classiest strip club in the city, but not the worst either (use *DH*, p. 259, for reference). Edom recruited him when a shady business deal in England went wrong; given a choice between arrest and a prison sentence, or informing for MI6, he took the one that got him back home as quickly as possible.

These days, he regrets the decision. It's not that Edom asks too much of him — one of its handlers swings by the club every few months with questions about Bucharest's underworld, and he has a number to call if he sees anything unusual — but since Sandu started paying attention, he's seen too much weirdness for him to sleep soundly. Without knowing what he was really doing, he's taken sides in an invisible war, and he worries that he's a foot soldier for the losing side.

Cop Talk is the best way to deal with Sandu — best not to remind him of the weird shit. He'll talk about various elements of Bucharest's criminal circuit, pointing to the Romanian Mafia (*DH*, p.

157), the Drug Boss (***DH***, p. 113), and the Human Trafficker (***DH***, p. 118). He knows which mafia gangs are on top, and which ones are desperate. A **Reassurance** spend and a lot of drink gets him to talk about other matters — maybe about the German woman (***DH***, p. 62), about the orphanage (***DH***, p. 223), about the old hospital (***DH***, p. 230).

Sandu can also offer a safe house (***DH***, p. 258), or provide untraceable cash or weapons (through the Arms Runner; ***DH***, p. 102) — but he'll want a big favor in return.

Unreliable: As above, but Sandu's in deep with some criminal syndicates or other factions — Edom's just one of his many masters, and it's not obvious which way he'll jump. At the very least, he's in debt to the Romanian Mafia (***DH***, p. 157) and under investigation by the Bucharest Street Cop (***DH***, p. 108). He might also be reporting to the SRI (***DH***, p. 156), the CIA's Station Bucharest (***DH***, p. 109), or even a rival vampire program (***DH***, p. 75).

Criminology or **Human Terrain** works out which of his masters has the tightest hold on him — he'll report everyone else's secrets to them, but won't betray theirs. The Agents can either work out a way to get more leverage over Sandu, or else **Intimidate** him for immediate results. The latter option burns him as a contact.

Traitorous: Sandu's got new friends — better friends. Undying friends. Two options present themselves.

First, Sandu may simply have fallen in with some elements of the Conspiracy, and told them everything he knows. He has no idea that he's an Edom asset, and believes he's reporting to the exoteric MI6, not the fabled Research Operations division. In this case, the Conspiracy is unlikely to make much use of Sandu, other than have him feed false information back to the British. **Criminology** or **Research** poke holes in Sandu's intel; **Tradecraft** guesses he's been flipped.

The second option's much nastier, but has a bigger payoff. Sandu has no idea he's reporting to Edom, but Dracula's mole in Edom knows who Sandu is. So, now the Conspiracy has an Edom asset in their pocket. It knows that anything it tells Sandu will go straight to the analysts at Ring, varnished with the conviction of innocence. It'll therefore use Sandu to lay traps for Edom. If the Agents survive one of these death traps, then **Tradecraft** coupled with **Bullshit Detector** or **Interrogation** tells them that Sandu isn't aware of how he's being used — he doesn't know he was Edom, so how could he have revealed that secret to his Conspiracy allies? The only logical inference is that someone within Edom tipped the Conspiracy off to Sandu's status.

Alternate Names: Ion Grigoraș, Francisc ("call me Frankie") Márton, Pietro Bellacqua (running the club for the Camorra)

Alternate Descriptions: (1) early 60s, short white hair, puffy pink face, immense mohair greatcoat

(2) mid-50s, square head with thick brown hair coated in product, immense arms and chest and hands, red-yellow-blue patriotic Romanian Olympic wrestling track suit

(3) mid-30s, sallow complexion, wiry build, scar over eye, really expensive Paris-cut suits

Defining Quirks: (1) twitchy eye or nose (nascent drug habit); (2) squeezes free hand into fist; (3) hisses sibilants and talks through his nose (old sinus or throat injury)

Investigative Abilities: Languages (English, Italian), Streetwise

General Abilities: Athletics 8, Hand-to-Hand 8, Shooting 2, Weapons 4

Alertness Modifier: +1

Stealth Modifier: −1

CHURCH SCAVENGER

Name: Maggie Canter

Role: Occult and religious informant

Description: early 40s, heavyset, reddish hair, dresses like a nun, smokes like a chimney

Stalwart: Canter runs Canter Antiques & Salvage, a large junk shop in East London. Over the years, the business has come to specialize in architecture and furniture salvaged from churches and other religious institutions. If you want to outfit your hipster bar with a few pews from a demolished church, or are looking to buy a load of old-fashioned bedsheets and tablecloths from a nunnery that ran out of nuns, Canter's is the place to go. She jokes that she's just finishing up what Henry the Eighth started with the destruction of the monasteries; these days, she makes regular trips to Ireland (*DH*, p. 235) to acquire new stock. In addition to her line in second-hand religious supplies, her junk shop and her extended family do a little bit of everything — rare books, graveyard groundskeeping and maintenance, nightclub security, maybe even the occasional *quasi-legal* bit of breaking-and-entering.

Edom employs her to look out for potentially useful relics — who knows where a copy of the *Zohar* of Moses de León (*DH*, p. 285) or Kate Reed's Diary (*DH*, p. 271) is going to show up? She also reports to them about unusual activity in London's graveyards and occult circles — she knows enough to keep an eye on the graves of suicides, and to pay attention to the movement of rats and wild dogs at sunset, and to count the number of kids drinking cans of cider in the shade of certain overgrown tombs in case one goes missing for a few hours.

She suspects that she's reporting to Edom, but keeps her mouth shut. It's about the only topic she does stay quiet about — Canter has opinions on everything else under the sun. Sifting through her nicotine-and-coffee-fueled diatribes with **Occult Studies** or **Criminology** may turn up useful information. Canter shies away from any deeper involvement with the occult, or with Edom. The supernatural, she says, is more trouble than it's worth. She only accepts money from Edom when she has to — her motivation is ideological, even religious, not mercenary.

Unreliable: As above, only Canter's more of a player. She knows the true value of certain relics; if she does happen across, say, Renfield's Journal (*DH*, p. 277) or a Vial of Blood (*DH*, p. 284) or even an Earthquake Device (*DH*, p. 266), she won't automatically give it to Edom. Now, the Crown can get in line with the other potential bidders — she knows the Sculptor (*DH*, p. 100) and the Art Forecaster (*DH*, p. 103), as well as the Psychic (*DH*, p. 96), and can beat the drums to attract the attention of one or two rival vampire programs (*DH*, p. 75) too ... **Negotiation** may be able to convince her to sell to Edom above any other buyer, but she's already attracted the attention of Edom's foes.

Traitorous: As above, but Canter's found something of real value. Take your pick from Le Dragon Noir (**DH**, p. 273; found in the attic of an old parish house in Dublin), a Sealed Coffin (**DH**, p. 278; recovered when the NHS demolished a small chapel on the grounds of Seward's asylum), a Knife Set (**DH**, p. 272; pawned and lost by the alcoholic uncle of the present Lord Holmwood — and there's something hidden beneath the velvet lining), a Vial of Blood (**DH**, p. 284; among the effects of an old pharmacy in Whitechapel), or the Westenra Brooch (**DH**, p. 284; stolen from Lucy's corpse and sold many times since then). She's decided to cut Edom out and exploit the powers of the relic herself. If she's very lucky, maybe she only gets herself killed, and **Forensic Pathology** can help identity the nature of the killer. It's also possible she gets inducted into the Conspiracy or otherwise enslaved by Dracula, or accidentally turns herself into a vampiric monster.

Alternate Names: Englebert Jessup, Philip Lockridge, Susan Wallis

Alternate Descriptions: (1) late 50s, thinning black hair, prominent Adam's apple and nose on skull-like head, wears clerical blacks with no collar

(2) early 20s, tattooed with Bible verses and thickly whiskered, skinny jeans and Doc Martens, floppy-brimmed porkpie hat

(3) mid-40s, well-put-together brunette, green eyes, vintage jeans and leather jacket, archbishop's ring on ring finger

Defining Quirks: (1) says "God's blood" and "God's wounds" as casual profanity; (2) uses a folded-over pectoral cross as a money clip; (3) makes sign of the cross in benediction at the end of conversations

Investigative Abilities:
Art History, Forgery
General Abilities: Driving 4, Infiltration 2, Preparedness 3
Alertness Modifier: +1
Stealth Modifier: +0

FARMER

Name: Petra Gabor
Role: Safe house Operator/Observer
Description: mid-60s, bent and tired, yellowed eyes, always has a big dog at her side

Stalwart: The black volcanic soil, watered with the blood of invaders, was fertile enough for them to risk living in the shadow of Castle Dracula. For years, they were precarious neighbors of the Count, and knew to stay indoors on certain nights and hang garlic from every window. It wasn't enough — the Count's Ruvari Szgany stole an infant girl out of her crib and brought her to the Castle, and killed her mother when she went looking for it a month later. On that night the Gabor family vowed eternal vengeance on Dracula.

The following year, the Englishmen came, and put an end to the Count, denying the Gabors the justice they sought. A few years after that, though, another Englishman came to visit them. He said his name was Alvah, and that he too was an enemy of the Count. That he would pay them to keep watch on the ruins.

They took his money, but it was still revenge that drove them.

The Gabors have been Edom assets in an unbroken line since 1902.

Their association with Edom has waxed and waned over the decades, especially after WWII and the Communist takeover of Romania, but they remember. Their isolated farmstead hasn't changed much in a hundred years. They have carefully avoided any entanglements that might attract undue attention; they have a bad

reputation among the other locals. No one of good heart, they whisper, would willingly live in that haunted valley. Petra Gabor is the current head of the family; her two sons and her younger daughter also live on the farm. Her oldest girl is in the Romanian armed forces. She works the land, as her ancestors did before her; her husband should be buried in the local graveyard, but she had his body brought to the Cenușa crematorium in Bucharest. The dead don't keep their secrets in this region.

Recontact them with **Tradecraft**, and old Petra can answer any two questions about Conspiracy activity at Castle Dracula, or provide a Safe House (**DH**, p. 258) for Agents on the run.

If Elvis hasn't reactivated the Gabors, it's because he fears they're under observation by Dracula's agents. Note that if you're using **The Hawkins Papers**, the second-last Flash Transmission (Paper 27) mentions that the "Borgo Watchers" were arrested — were there other watchers, or did Petra's father somehow bargain his way out of prison?

Unreliable: The Gabors lost contact with Edom in 1978; their handler was one of those arrested by the Securitate and carried off to Pitești Prison (**DH**, p. 218). As Edom can't be sure if the handler gave away the names of the Gabors under torture, the family can no longer be considered reliable.

Petra's father told her to watch for the sign of the cup-and-drop, and gave her a few Edom recognition codes (p. 46). He also warned her that the English are drawn to Castle Dracula like moths to a flame, and there will be more killing before the end. Reactivating Petra as an asset requires a **Reassurance** spend (not to mention forty years of back pay).

Traitorous: It was a century-long bluff. The Gabors weren't the family who lost a mother and a child — they were the ones who *stole* the baby and gave it to the Count as an offering. The mother was the wife of one of their farm laborers. She was torn apart by wolves, but his bones lie buried with many, many others under the Gabors' farmyard. When Edom came sniffing for clues about the Count, the loyal Gabors were only too willing to volunteer as informants.

Bullshit Detector isn't going to work here; they've lived their cover for a century. Maybe a heavy rainstorm could bring some more recent remains to the surface, to be identified with **Forensic Pathology**, or a lot of **Research** and **Traffic Analysis** might confirm that the Gabors have misled every Alvah from 1902 to the present day.

Alternate Names: Magda Ungur, Elena Ștefănescu, Katerina Popescu

Alternate Descriptions: (1) late 50s, broad build, layers of dresses and aprons, holds a sharp-looking carving knife

(2) early 40s, once beautiful face slowly thickening and coarsening with age and unceasing farm labor, jeans and work shirt, calloused hands

(3) mid-20s, black hair and eyes, peasant dress, head covered with a scarf, an even bigger dog

Defining Quirks: (1) only drinks milk; (2) makes eye contact with oldest male Agent and holds it throughout the conversation; (3) earthy, ribald sense of humor about less than appropriate matters

Investigative Abilities: Human Terrain (Borgo Pass), Languages (English, Hungarian, Slovak), Notice

General Abilities: Surveillance 4 (if still active), Weapons 4

Alertness Modifier: +1
Stealth Modifier: +0

ROMANIAN MORTICIAN

Name: Dumitra Skarlat

Role: Medical and morbidity expert in Bucharest

Description: late 20s, vampire-pale, unexpectedly wide grin, hums while she works

Stalwart: Skarlat works as an assistant medical examiner in the morgue at one of Bucharest's larger hospitals. She keeps tabs on unexpected or unusual deaths in the city for Edom. Elvis recruited her after her brother Tomas died in mysterious circumstances; he's dropped hints that something supernatural was responsible, and that Skarlat can help track the monster down. She thinks he's some sort of Van Helsing–esque vampire slayer, and is unaware of any connection to Edom.

She may provide similar off-the-books information or be hopelessly in love with the Bucharest Street Cop (**DH**, p. 108); she might be a supporter of the cause of the Dissident (**DH**, p. 112), hoping to find meaning in a struggle against the state; she might take a mystic view of death, or troll the gullible lunatics — in either case, she's a regular on the Online Mystic's (**DH**, p. 126) board.

If Elvis doesn't provide an introduction, then **Vampirology** or **Occult Studies** plus **Reassurance** convinces her that you're on the side of the angels. She can get access to death records and autopsy reports, but anything more may require forward progress on finding Tomas' killer.

Unreliable: Skarlat's not going to wait for Elvis to solve Tomas' death — she's determined to do it herself. She's hired the Bucharest Private Detective (**DH**, p. 107) to investigate Tomas' last days, and she's following up his leads by herself. **Notice** picks up on her nervous energy — and the scratches on her hands and knees, suggesting she's been sneaking into places where she shouldn't go.

Her next lead takes her to (pick one) Strasba Orphanage (**DH**, p. 223), Pitești Prison (**DH**, p. 218), Čachtice Castle (**DH**, p. 245) or the secret location of the "Black Light" site (**DH**, p. 204). Worse — from Edom's point of view — she's got details about Elvis' cover identity and the time and place of their next meet up on her phone. If she's caught, she will jeopardize the Duke.

Traitorous: Dumitra knows exactly what happened to Tomas: she killed him as an offering to the Lord of the Dead. It was on St. Andrew's Eve in 2012 when every corpse in her morgue sat up, crowned in blue flame, and spoke with one voice — the voice of the Master. Now, she's turned her section of the morgue into a latter-day version of the Munich Dead House (*DH*, p. 226), a necromantic engine through which Dracula can interrogate the recently deceased. The Count (or one of his minions) has fed from Dumitra; **Vampirology** spots the behavior changes; **Diagnosis** spots the puncture wounds concealed beneath flesh-tone bandages.

Alternate Names: Nina Odobleja, Anton Teclu, Ruxandra Valentinu

Alternate Descriptions: (1) mid-30s, slightly overweight, short bobbed brown hair

(2) early 40s, thin build, mordant expression, thick shock of black hair

(3) early 30s, blonde, Goth-purple makeup, very attractive and knows it

Defining Quirks: (1) long, restless fingers; (2) scratches herself between the eyebrows (is that hair growing there?); (3) tip of tongue protrudes while she thinks

Investigative Abilities:
Diagnosis, Forensic Pathology, Pharmacy, Vampirology

General Abilities: Filch 3, Medic 4
Alertness Modifier: +1
Stealth Modifier: +0

SAILOR

Name: Jurgen Offermans

Role: Informant within HGD Shipping

Description: late 40s, bearded and weathered, missing two fingers on left hand, vapes instead of smokes but isn't happy about it.

Stalwart: Offermans is a cargo engineer on various freighters operating out of the Netherlands. He's an uncomplicated, thorough man — get the cargo on safe, keep it safe, unload it safe, then go out on the town and get drunk. When he was younger, his plan was to put money aside and maybe start his own business or have a family, but he never got around to that, and now he feels too old to change. Everything has its place aboard ship, even him.

Offermans knows that some cargos are unusual. Bad luck, even — he's not superstitious, but he's good at spotting patterns. Knows that when they're carrying one of those containers, there'll be bad dreams all night, and bad weather, and that there'll be rats on board no matter how much poison he lays down. Big rats that climb up on the container and look down at him, like they're watching him.

If Edom runs HGD Shipping (*DH*, p. 145), then Offermans has been with the company long enough to be considered reliable, and so is assigned to freight runs involving Special Biological Assets. Edom knows that he'll keep his eyes open and won't dismiss any strange events out of hand, but also won't talk to anyone outside the company. **Bureaucracy** and the presentation of HGD documentation get him talking; **Reassurance** might be needed if he saw something very strange.

If HGD Shipping is a Conspiracy cut-out, then Elvis has recruited Offermans as an asset — he met the sailor in a bar, bought him a few drinks, and got him talking. Elvis has a contingency plan in place to solidify his hold over Offermans if necessary (plant drugs, have a bribed cop arrest Offermans, then smooth the whole incident over), but he'll only make that play if he needs more than casual gossip out of his informant. If the Agents put that plan into operation, then **Negotiation** or **Intimidation** gets Offermans talking.

In addition to information about HGD activities and odd rumors from the Black Sea (**Streetwise**), Offermans can help smuggle cargo (or people) untraceably from the UK or Netherlands to any port on the Black Sea.

Alternate Descriptions: (1) early 30s, blond and sunburnt, tall and gangly

(2) mid-30s, stocky, already balding but shaves his head to hide it, watch cap and pea jacket, hand-rolls his smokes

(3) late 40s, dark and ferret-faced, short, old Royal Navy surplus jacket, chews tobacco

Defining Quirks: (1) spits to punctuate emphatic sentences; (2) becomes visibly depressed while drinking; (3) swings arms while on shore, keeps hands in pockets on shipboard

Investigative Abilities: Languages (English, Russian), Streetwise

General Abilities: Conceal 5, Hand-to-Hand 4, Mechanics 6, Weapons 2

Alertness Modifier: +1

Stealth Modifier: +0

(+1 on shipboard)

Unreliable: As above, but Offermans has fallen into the orbit of someone undesirable from Edom's perspective. It might be labor organizer and political firebrand Geerd Hoorn (*DH*, p. 45), or he's found a new cause with the Dissident (*DH*, p. 112). Maybe Offermans is in debt to the Drug Boss (*DH*, p. 113) or some other criminal figure. In any case, the Agents must dismantle this association before they can exploit Offermans as an asset — **Interrogation** may be needed to find out exactly who needs to be … indulged.

Traitorous: As Unreliable, but Offermans' new friend is connected to the Conspiracy or a rival vampire program. It's using him to help cover up their operations at sea (shipping vampires and/or victims overseas, abducting Edom SBA containers, sinking Edom ships). **Traffic Analysis** or **Electronic Surveillance** uncovers Offermans' connection to the threat.

Alternate Names: Claus Hestbæk [Danish], Stanislaw Zieminski [Polish], Jean Aquilina [Maltese]

SOCIAL WORKER

Name: Neela Chaudri

Role: Monitor for Edom's psychic early warning network

Description: mid-30s, Indian, long hair in a tight bun, always has a coffee cup in hand

Stalwart: Chaudri works — or thinks she works — for a pilot program run these days by the National Mental Health Development Unit, although the program itself dates back to the 1970s and the early days of Care in the Community. The aim is to take patients suffering from moderate psychiatric problems — nonviolent schizophrenics, mostly — and settle them in small, often isolated rural communities in the hopes that the more sedate surroundings will promote healing. Chaudri's job is to travel the whole country, interviewing these patients and adjusting their medication. Every month, she transcribes her notes and observations, collates the report, and sends it into an NHS Centre in Plaistow. No one ever seems to take any notice of it, and when she rang up to complain to her supervisors about the lack of support, she was told to keep quiet or she'd endanger her job.

Buy her a coffee in one of the motorway service stations that have become her second home, use **Reassurance** (or **Diagnosis** to prove your credentials), and she'll talk at length.

In her private opinion, this program is nonsense. These poor patients need round-the-clock care, instead of being housed in *lighthouses* and disused naval bases and other strange places. Why are so many of them on the *coast* anyway? Why in heaven is she supposed to take *compass readings* when interviewing them, especially if they get agitated? Why the interest in their dreams?

In fact, Neela works for a program instituted by Edom in 1977 as part of Operation Piper (**DH**, p. 333), the psychic research unit created in consultation with the Psychic (**DH**, p. 96). Her patients are located at strategic ports along England's coast (Cruden Bay (**DH**, p. 176), Whitby (**DH**, p. 177), Other Ports (**DH**, p. 172), Exeter (**DH**, p. 167) — all near current or former Chain Home Deep listening posts). Her reports get filed in the Edom archives; a combination of **Traffic Analysis** coupled with **Occult Studies** and maybe **Cryptography** could pull useful information from the noise, but no one reads the reports these days.

The Madman (**DH**, p. 121) and "Cushing" (**DH**, p. 92) may be among her patients.

Unreliable: As above, but this version of Chaudri has lost patience for the program. No one reads her reports or does anything with them, so why should she bother writing them? She's sent in exactly the same report, modulo a few small changes, every month for the last two years. She still delivers medications to her patients, and interviews them out of boredom, but she just dumps her notes unread into the trash.

These scribbled notes might be found and passed on to the Tabloid Journalist (**DH**, p. 134), the Online Mystic (**DH**, p. 126), the Psychic (**DH**, p. 96) — or even some stringer for a rival vampire program, like the Turkish Agent (**DH**, p. 136), Chinese Agent (**DH**, p. 110), or Retired KGB Agent (**DH**, p. 97). **Interrogation** gets Chaudri to admit her negligence and give the Agents a place to start looking for the missing interview transcripts.

Traitorous: The Madman (**DH**, p. 121) is one of Chaudri's patients — and she's one of his victims. He attacked her, brought her to an isolated location (perhaps a deserted Hillingham (**DH**, p. 190) or Coldfall House (**DH**, p. 188)) and left her there, tied up and bleeding.

And a vampire found her.

Chaudri's now a Renfield, serving her vampiric master. Her new mission is to infiltrate Operation Edom. She intends to start seeding interesting details in her reports, and make enough noise that she'll get noticed by the Dukes. Once she has their attention, the next step is to

DIRECTOR'S BRIEFING ■ HUNTING THE DOSSIER

get upgraded from a mere szohordok to someone on the inside, maybe a place on Edom's scientific staff ...

Bullshit Detector picks up that Chaudri has an ulterior motive, but it'll take **Diagnosis** plus **Vampirology** to work out that she's a Renfield, as she's got the medical expertise to conceal most of her symptoms.

Alternate Names: Viola McGuire, Mary Torrance, David Jones

Alternate Descriptions: (1) mid-20s, sweaters and slacks, large round glasses [first civil service job out of university]

(2) late 50s, pantsuit and professional cosmetics, grim expression [time-serving until her pension]

(3) late 30s, cheap blazer and jeans, pale complexion and dark hair, always looks rumpled and a bit lost

Defining Quirks: (1) keeps a paper appointment book instead of putting it in her phone; (2) clucks tongue while looking at a document or making a decision; (3) moves arms and legs with unconscious grace (childhood dance lessons)

Investigative Abilities: Diagnosis, Pharmacy, Reassurance
General Abilities: Medic 4, Shrink 4
Alertness Modifier: +0
Stealth Modifier: –1

THE FIELDS OF EDOM

He calleth to me out of Mount Seir, "Watchman, what of the night? Watchman, what of the night?" The watchman said, "The morning cometh, and also the night: if ye will inquire, inquire ye: return and return again."

— Isaiah 21:11–12, on the burden of Edom

In this campaign frame, the players take on the roles of second-tier Edom operatives. They're Edom's troubleshooters, one step down from the Dukes. There's a problem — the Dracula Dossier has fallen into the wrong hands, and it must be retrieved, the leak plugged. The real danger, though, isn't the thieves who stole it; it's the possibility that they'll get themselves killed, and the vampires will obtain that Dossier and use it to break free of Edom's control. The Agents must find the Dossier before that happens.

For the dead travel fast, but not faster than a holy bullet with an allicin-cyanide hollow-point.

HUNTING THE DOSSIER

"Hopkins" (**DH**, p. 117), whoever he or she is, got hold of the Dracula Dossier as per the standard campaign setup and passed it onto the Opposition (p. 104). Prince (p. 76), Edom's in-house hacker, picked up on the tail end of the Internet traffic between "Hopkins" and the Opposition.

At the start of the campaign, give the players a copy of the annotated **Dracula Unredacted**. If you give them a physical copy, then that's the copy from MI6's archives that "Hopkins" annotated and scanned. If you give them an electronic copy, then that's the file that Prince intercepted as it was sent to the Opposition. Either way, it's the biggest security leak since 1977.

The Agents must:

■ retrieve and destroy any copies of the Dossier
■ find out who "Hopkins" is, and apprehend him or her
■ find out who received the Dossier, and deal with them as required

- ensure that the leak of the Dossier does not interfere with Edom's counter-terror program
- contain any fallout from the leak

From that point on, the running of the operation is up to the players. Do they follow up on clues from the Dossier, in the hopes of intercepting the Opposition before it breaks into Edom's secrets? ("*We'll put a watch on the old Carfax base — that's where I'd look first.*") Do they try exploring the annotations, so they can identify and find "Hopkins"? Do they wait for the Opposition to make the first move? It's still an improvised campaign, but the players' mission is very different.

HEAT

The usual rules on Heat still apply, even though the Agents are technically working for MI6. Abroad, they need to dodge foreign counterespionage agencies and the police. In the UK, they need to avoid dragging Edom into the public eye. The various Dukes offer ways to remove Heat not normally available to *Night's Black Agents* characters.

If an Agent's Heat ever rises above that character's Bureaucracy *rating* (not current pool), then Edom may decide to cut its losses and either burn that Agent, or issue an indulgence order (p. 27).

THE OPPOSITION

Who has the Dossier? Who's trying to break Edom? The answer to that question might change over the course of the campaign as the threat escalates. Some possibilities are described below. Of course, any of these groups might use hired muscle, proxies, false flags, or other allies instead of attacking Edom directly. Think about player characters in a regular *Night's Black Agents* game, who might whistle up Serbian gangsters with a Network spend in one operation, then disguise themselves as American mercenaries in the next.

Rogues: Standard *Night's Black Agents* player characters, in other words; a group of burned spies, ex-criminals, and shady black ops types who have a grudge against vampires. While this is a wonderfully meta approach to the Opposition ("You're playing against player characters"), the downside is that rogue spies don't have many low-level mooks to beat up. Rogues are an excellent starting Opposition, but once the player characters eliminate two or three members of the original group, cut the throats of the rest in some alleyway in Bucharest and have a bigger bad guy faction take the Dossier.

Rival Spies: The CIA. The Russian FSB. The German BND. Mossad. The Romanian SIE. Even MI5. Edom has many enemies in the espionage world who are eager to steal its secrets and gain control of its vampire assets — or to shut it down for good. These groups have no direct experience in dealing with vampires, but the Dracula Dossier hands them the keys to the kingdom.

Non-State Actors: Organized crime (the Romanian Mafia; *DH*, p. 157), corporations (maybe the Petroleum Executive (*DH*, p. 127) wants to secure Romania's oil fields with Dracula's help, or perhaps a biotech company believes it can monetize vampirism), crazy dying billionaires who want to cheat death, Nazi death cults, the Caldwell Foundation (*DH*, p. 160) …

Counterparts: Edom-like factions within other espionage agencies — the German vampire program (*DH*, p. 75) that made Orlok (*DH*, p. 70), perhaps, or the CIA vampire initiative started after 1977 (*DH*, p. 76). They've coveted Edom's secrets for decades, and now they intend to use the Dossier to break the British operation wide open and take everything of value. These counterparts may have their own supernatural assets or augmented agents like Jacks.

Renegade Edom Operatives: Disgraced ex-Edom operatives kicked out after the mole hunt, burnt-out Jacks who now serve the Master, retired Dukes suffering from an attack of conscience, or an escaped Edom vampire running her own counter-operation.

Dracula: If Edom's running Dracula, then the last thing it wants is its old playbook falling into the Count's hands. With the Dossier, Dracula could send his minions to attack or subvert key Edom targets, ripping his prison apart from the inside. Alternatively, his goal may be to gain control of Edom. With his supposed controllers under his control, the Count could act freely in England, shielded against suspicion or interference by those who are supposed to keep him in check.

Another Supernatural Threat: Dracula isn't the only vampire out there. Perhaps the Linea Dracula vampires (see the *Night Black Agents* rulebook) plan to free their progenitor from Edom's control. Could be Lilith (*DH*, p. 69), or Zalmoxic cultists (*DH*, p. 289). Maybe a vengeful, immortal Mina Harker is finally making her play to bring down Edom. Maybe Dracula's Satanic conspiracy (*DH*, p. 55) is still at large, even if Dracula's no longer running the show. The Solomonari (*DH*, p. 74) would be a weird outta-left-field threat, but could be fun and terrifying foes.

An Escalating Threat: "Hopkins" leaks the Dossier to a band of rogue operatives. They get killed by the FSB, but it turns out that a corrupt FSB officer sold the Dossier to the Romanian mafia, who are secretly under the control of Dracula. The Opposition changes and escalates over the course of the campaign. Swap the Opposition every time you move up a level on the Oppyramid.

No Single Actor: For a more episodic campaign, "Hopkins" pulls a Snowden and uploads the Dossier to a public site, where anyone can access it. So, one week the Agents have to protect Edom assets in Romania from Dracula's minions in the Romanian mafia; next week, it's off to Turkey to stop the Milli İstihbarat Teşkilatı from digging up things they shouldn't unearth under Tokat Castle.

THE OPPYRAMID

The Oppyramid works just like the Vampyramid — it's a tiered menu of plot twists and enemy actions that the Director can throw in as needed. In this case, it models the actions of the Opposition as it uses the stolen Dossier to bring down Edom.

In addition, the Conspiracy Vampyramid from page 18 of the ***Director's Handbook*** still applies to a *Fields of Edom* campaign. When Dracula's working with Edom, stick to the responses like *Quid Pro Quo* (***DH***, p. 18) or *Burn and Freeze* (***DH***, p. 19) — although of course, the Agents might be obliged to cover up a *Probing Attack* (***DH***, p. 18) or a *Massacre* (***DH***, p. 20). Later in the campaign, if the Agents get burned or if Dracula breaks faith with Edom, you can use all the weapons in the Conspiracy's arsenal on top of the problems thrown out by the Oppyramid.

ROW ONE: SURFACE DETAILS

Uncover Node: The Opposition runs a surveillance operation on an Edom false front or Conspiracy node. It might start following Axel Logistics (***DH***, p. 141) delivery vehicles carrying sensitive Edom material, or start investigating Heal the Children (***DH***, p. 150). The Agents need to either disrupt the surveillance operation or convince the watchers that the node is wholly innocent; if they fail, the node will be exposed and the Opposition will be much closer to Edom's secrets.

Break-In: The Opposition attempts to break into a secondary Edom or Conspiracy facility — maybe the Strasba Orphanage (***DH***, p. 223), Hillingham (***DH***, p. 190), or Leutner Fabrichen (***DH***, p. 146). The Agents must either protect the facility or ensure that the Opposition comes away empty handed.

Interrogate Contact: Someone with knowledge of Edom's past or current operations goes missing. Were they kidnapped by the Opposition, or have they switched sides? Either way, find them before they reveal what they know. Good candidates include the Defector (***DH***, p. 93), the Bureaucrat (***DH***, p. 108), the SRI Agent in Charge (***DH***, p. 133), or any of the MI5 or MI6 contacts.

Black Bag Job: The Opposition plants a spying device at a key Edom site, or hacks into the group's secure internal network, or convinces a low-level Edom asset to pass on information to it. The Agents need to find the bug or plug the leak. Possible targets include the Norman Shaw Buildings (***DH***, p. 193), Exeter (***DH***, p. 167), a researcher at Seward's Asylum (***DH***, p. 195), or a contact within the British police or the SRI.

Perturb Ally: An ally of Edom — a politician, a criminal leader, a scientist, a Conspiracy node, a Legacy — starts acting oddly. Are they nervous about the Opposition finding out about their involvement? The Agents need to convince the ally that everything is under control and the Opposition isn't a threat to them. This requires both a **Reassurance** spend and proof that the danger's been dealt with. Maybe they've already been targeted or blackmailed — or even flipped — by the Opposition. Maybe the ally panics or does something stupid in response to being targeted that the Agents need to clean up. Targets for such an operation include a Godalming Legacy (***DH***, pp. 43–44),

the Petroleum Executive (***DH***, p. 127), staff at NIEP (***DH***, p. 151), the Tabloid Journalist (***DH***, p. 134) or one of the banks (Klopstock & Billreuth (***DH***, p. 145) or Burdett's (***DH***, p. 143)).

Disrupt Ongoing Operation: The Opposition attacks an ongoing Edom operation — a vampire hunt, a payment run to agents in Romania, an exercise in mapping telluric currents, or some other quotidian-for-a-secret–spy agency–with-vampires activity. The Agents need to rescue the survivors, salvage the operation, and secure it against further Opposition attack.

ROW TWO: DIGGING

Contagion: The Opposition transmits a copy of the Dossier to a third party. This might be done deliberately (leaking it to the Journalist (***DH***, p. 120) or the Icelandic Diplomat (***DH***, p. 119)), accidentally (it's recovered by the Bucharest Street Cop (***DH***, p. 108) or the Medievalist (***DH***, p. 122)), or it's stolen from the Opposition by someone (the CIA Agent (***DH***, p. 91), the Hildesheim Legacy (***DH***, p. 116) and his Mossad connections, or Dracula's Conspiracy). The Agents must recover this second copy of the Dossier before someone else becomes a player in the game.

The Family Jewels: The Opposition steals something vital to Edom. It must be recovered immediately. Excellent candidates include a Vial of Blood (***DH***, p. 284), *Le Dragon Noir* (***DH***, p. 273), Renfield's Journal (***DH***, p. 277), an Earthquake Device (***DH***, p. 266)— or maybe it kidnaps a vital Legacy. The Opposition starts to make use of its prize immediately. If it grabs *Le Dragon Noir,* then one of them tries to become a vampire. If it's got an earthquake machine, then it sends the device to Romania to triangulate on Dracula's Castle, or starts smashing Edom buildings with it.

Lay a Trap: The Opposition trails evidence that it's planning an attack on Edom, but it's a trap — the intent is to ambush and kill the Agents. Possible vectors: a raid on an Edom operating base overseas (in Argentina or Ireland), theft of a vampire-related artifact (perhaps an Aytown painting from the Pinakothek (*DH*, p. 228) or *Le Dragon Noir* (*DH*, p. 273)). When the Agents get there, hit them with as much force as the Opposition can muster.

Flip Ally: Using material from the Dossier or stolen in a previous attack on Edom, the Opposition flips one of Edom's allies — a Conspiracy node, a key NPC like a retired MI6 officer, or maybe even a Duke or a Legacy. Once the Agents discover this betrayal, they need to decide how to react — eliminate the ally, try to flip them back, feed them bad intelligence.

Alternatively, the Opposition might approach one of the player characters.

Eyeless in Gaza: The Opposition disrupts Edom's surveillance and intelligence-gathering apparatus in a key area. It might crash part of the CCTV network, eliminate an Edom shell team at just the wrong moment, flip an asset-in-place and get him or her to feed false data to Edom for weeks (*"Hey, why has our man in Munich sent exactly the same report, word for word, for six reports?"*), or just cause a massive distraction like a terrorist attack. The Agents are temporarily deprived of a source of information they've previously relied upon, and need to get on the ground and find out what's really going on.

ROW THREE: STRIKE

Check to the King: The Opposition hires a criminal team to capture one of Edom's Dukes, or a similarly important figure in the organization, like an Edom-aligned Legacy, "Dr. Drawes," or even Edom's vampire. The Agents have only a brief window to execute a rescue — or is this just a feint, and the Opposition's real target is elsewhere?

Release Horror: The Opposition unearths some supernatural horror that Edom contained or defeated in the past (or maybe Edom discovered it and chose not to exploit it). The Agents now need to track down and destroy the monster, guided by Edom's old field reports and the testimony of retired former officers, before old sins come back to roost.

Pass the Chalice: The Opposition hits at the next generation of Edom. Possible vectors — passing a copy of the Dossier onto a young Legacy like Billie Harker (*DH*, p. 42), forcing the Agents to justify all of Edom's past actions or lose the Legacy's faith; poisoning the current batch of Seward Serum, incapacitating or killing Edom's Jacks; flipping a contact or subordinate that the player characters regularly rely on.

Flip Patron: The Opposition flips a major ally of Edom. Some possibilities — MI6 disowns Edom and tries to shut the operation down; an Opposition-friendly politician begins a parliamentary investigation into Edom; the CIA tries to take charge of vampire handling; one of Edom's Dukes switches sides or gets bought off.

ROW FOUR: CHAOS

Disrupt Core Operation: The Opposition strikes at one of Edom's core activities, using supernatural means or extreme force. The obvious target here is the ongoing War on Terror — maybe the Opposition takes out Dracula's handlers, so the Count is now hunting without supervision in some war-torn part of Iraq or Afghanistan — or London. The Agents need to find out how Edom was compromised, and bring the vampiric asset back under Edom's control.

Eliminate Agent: The Opposition targets one of the player characters for assassination. If it has access to supernatural weapons, it'll send a vampire or some other monster to make the kill. If it's using mundane means, then it hires an elite assassin to do the job for it. At this stage in the campaign, up the stakes by having the attack happen in public, or at the Agent's Safety, or en route to an Edom facility.

Alternatively, kill a friendly Duke or two.

Burn Agents: Edom turns on the Agents, leaving them out in the cold. Has the Opposition somehow convinced the Dukes that the PCs are not to be trusted, or is this an internal power struggle within Edom? Either way, without the protection and resources of Edom, the Agents have nowhere to take shelter when all their old enemies come hunting for them. The Agents must fight their way back to the inside and discover why they were burned, then clear their names.

ROW FIVE: MORTAL WOUNDS

Burn Key Site: The Opposition attacks the heart of Edom — is it Ring, or HMS *Proserpine*, or even somewhere in Romania? Depending on your tastes, this might range from "a vampire loose in the hallowed halls of Ring, feasting on Dukes" to "helicopter gunships raining Hellfire missiles down on Castle Dracula." Unlike previous attacks on Edom, where the Agents come in afterwards to pick through the bones and salvage what they can, this time they're right in the middle of the action. Can they defend Edom's innermost sanctum?

Break the Seal: The Opposition destroys whatever hold Edom had over Dracula (or, if Edom wasn't using Dracula, then the Opposition resurrects the Count). Either way, Dracula himself is suddenly in play, and he's hungry ...

(Or, if not Dracula, then how about Countess Báthory (*DH*, p. 65) or Zalmoxis (*DH*, p. 289) ...)

ROW SIX: DESTRUCTION

Fall From Grace: Edom's shut down, its official sanction revoked. Its leadership dead, disgraced, or missing. The Agents are all that's left. They have a choice — do they walk away from the shadow world of vampires and conspiracies, and take some obscure desk jobs in the bowels of SIS for the rest of their lives? Do they switch sides and go after the vampires who betrayed them? Or do they go underground and keep faithful to the grand design that was set down all those years ago?

RUNNING THE CAMPAIGN—

Just because the players are on the inside of the Conspiracy doesn't mean that they know what's going on. Keep things as compartmentalized and secretive as you can — everything in Edom is on a need-to-know basis. The player characters might know all about vampire-hunting operations in London, and have visited HMS *Proserpine*, but have next to no idea about what's going on in Romania or further afield. Early in the campaign, keep the action focused on two or three Dukes and their respective domains — maybe the Agents are working with Hound and liaise with Prince and Tinman, or work for Oakes and get reports from Osprey and Elvis. Give them access to only a small corner of the Edom response pyramid. Make them feel cramped and surrounded by rivals and cutthroats. Holding their ground in Edom is hard enough, even before they start investigating leaks and vampires.

Unlike a regular **Night's Black Agents** campaign, where the Agents are renegades and rogues without any higher authority to report to, in this campaign the Agents have responsibilities to their superiors in Edom and the British state. They can break the law, but only when it is unavoidable or sanctioned by their masters. Make them consider the consequences of their actions: a bunch of burned spies can break into the Journalist's flat and interrogate her, but it's a different story and a different headline when MI6 officers intimidate a British journalist. Everything should be a compromise — success should require making enemies within Edom, or cutting deals that will come back to haunt them, or breaking their own moral codes. Use the first one or two sessions to lay the foundations of the campaign and teach the players the structure of Edom, to embed them in the grand edifice of the Secret Intelligence Service — and then use the next two or three to hammer cracks and break divisions in that structure.

The goal is to make the players feel the weight of Edom's history — they're not free agents, they're part of something bigger and older, heirs to all the operation's triumphs and sins.

USE THE DUKES

The Dukes serve multiple purposes in an Edom campaign. They embody the bureaucracy of Edom, giving the players a quick and easy map of the organization's power structure — Tyler, for example, is everything to do with domestic politics; he's the Duke you go to when you need political sanction and the Duke who complains when the Agents cause a diplomatic incident.

They're there to be mentors, nemeses, and rivals for the player characters. Ultimately, they may also be goals — either the Agents aspire to become replacement Dukes themselves when the current incumbents start dying, or they uncover evidence that one or more of the Dukes is a traitor.

They're there to be the recurring cast. Figures like "D" and "Dr. Drawes" are too remote and exalted to deal with the average player character; the other Edom personnel and assets are guest stars, showing up for a session or two and then sinking back into obscurity. The Dukes define how the players interact with Edom.

They're such important non-player characters to a *Fields of Edom* campaign that it's worth lavishing extra care on them. Find a voice or portrayal for each Duke; have a visual reminder like a prop or an ID photo for each one too.

BURY SECRETS

In a standard **Dracula Dossier** campaign, the players start with only a vague idea of what Edom is and how it works, based on the marginal hints in the Dossier and what they've picked up through osmosis from reading about the campaign online. Everything is up for grabs — Edom's headquarters might be at Ring, or Exeter, or London, or Bucharest. The operation might be an underfunded, fly-by-night black op without official action, or it might be running MI6. It's then up to the Director and players to discover the real state of Edom, clearing away the fog through improvisational play and investigation until the truth is revealed.

Fields of Edom must take a slightly different approach. While junior Edom officers won't have access to every detail of the operation — need-to-know only, dear boy — they do at least have a working knowledge of the sections they work in. Avoid locking yourself into a single interpretation of events and keep your improvisational options open by building in trapdoors of uncertainty. Early on, have the Agents discover some seemingly pointless or contradictory cover-up — maybe something like Dun Dreach-Fhola (**DH**, p. 235) has been erased from the archives, or a mentor-figure hints that they shouldn't believe a word written by one of the previous Dukes (and, as Edom tradition is to avoid distinguishing between one holder of a Dukedom and the next, that makes *everything* signed by that codename suspect ...). Sowing doubt early in the campaign frees you to reveal that everything the players know about Edom is wrong.

EDOM BY DAY

Edom is the player characters' day job, but they have lives outside it. Include a scene or two every session which explores the player characters' personal lives, their family and friends (especially if the Agents suffered a significant Stability loss that session). You can use these scenes to give an external perspective on Edom activities — they get to see what their cover-ups and intrigues look like from the outside. This gives them the conspiratorial frisson of knowing that, say, the recent fire in the London Underground was actually the destruction of Count Orlok, or who really pushed the Icelandic Diplomat over the falls at Barnafoss.

It's considered gauche to put a player character's dependent NPCs in jeopardy too often, but in a *Fields of Edom* campaign, it's almost obligatory. After all, you have the perfect literary antecedent; Dracula targeted the spouses and partners of his enemies in the novel, so you should do the same. If the Agents don't take steps to protect their loved ones and keep them hidden, they're fair game for attacks by Dracula, his minions, the Opposition, rival vampire programs, or even rival Dukes.

PREPARE TO BURN

Getting betrayed by or losing faith in your own organization is a staple of spy fiction, and there's a high chance that your Agents are going to go rogue at some point, either because of a "Burn Agents" Oppyramid reaction or on their own initiative. You can push them towards going rogue by giving them strong evidence, but not cast-iron proof, that a particular Duke is a servant of Dracula, then giving that Duke more and more influence in Edom. Even Agents loyal to Edom may decide that they can better serve the operation's ideals from a safe distance and a safe house.

Before the Agents get burned, give them cordwood and asbestos. Set up incidents that will justify their burning — past crimes, stains on their records, blood on their hands. Make sure there are reasons that they can't take their case to the authorities or to their superiors in Edom. You need to force them into the criminal underworld where regular **Nights Black Agents** player characters dwell, and ensure they can't come back to Edom easily.

Burning a character in the middle of a campaign, though, is much more traumatic and damaging than doing so as part of character generation and setup. It's one thing to say, *"Oh, my character used to work for SIS before she got burned,"* but something else entirely to play an SIS character for a dozen sessions, develop that character's supporting cast of friends, family, co-workers, and other recurrent contacts — and then tear all that away. It's much harder for player characters to run away, even when every point of **Tradecraft** and **Military Science** (not to mention **Sense Trouble**) tells them to. To make the transition easier, ensure that some of the characters' supporting cast have useful skills that can help with the first chaotic session after being burnt. Give them a sure-fire one-shot method of escaping Edom's dragnet (this may be an excellent time to move the campaign focus from England to Romania).

Agents who have been portrayed as being especially loyal, either to Edom as an institution or to a particular Duke or other individual within the organization, may need an extra push to get them to run when burned. Killing the object of their loyalty works very well.

THE REDEMPTION OF EDOM

It just may be possible, in a game of noble **Stakes**, to return Edom to its perhaps-original role as Britain's bulwark against the Un-Dead. The Agents discover who in Edom is corrupted by Dracula, and reveal his treason to someone: "D," on the off chance he's not irredeemably linked to the Dracula mission, or more likely a trustworthy MI6 or MI5 source they've uncovered during the campaign.

Agents interested in saving Edom from its own worst instincts need to do a few things as the campaign goes forward:

- Obtain as much actionable proof of Edom internal corruption as possible, ideally involving things that a Crown prosecutor will be willing to believe.
- Find a senior Duke who is provably innocent of the above charges, and ideally one who has not dealt directly with Dracula. If no such Duke exists, they may have to raise one of their own to such a position.
- Bring down, expose, or even eliminate corrupt Dukes and other senior Edom personnel.
- Take every opportunity to dust vampires, especially those who prey on the innocent.
- Destroy all Edom research on vampire containment or exploitation: the Seward Serum can nicely symbolize Edom's addiction to its supposed foes.
- Assist or amplify research in actual anti-vampire weaponry. Drawing the line between this goal and the above — how to research vampire killing without captive specimens? — can fill the Agents' discussions and planning.
- Make sure no actual terror attack gets through to Britain: the old Edom will happily blame it on the Agents interfering with the Montseir protocol, and come back stronger and more corrupt than ever.
- And of course — kill Dracula. As long as the King Vampire lives, he can always seduce Edom into trying to control him.

Redeeming Edom is likely a long-term continuing challenge (**NBA**, p. 50) of **Bureaucracy** with a Difficulty of 100 or more. Each successful mission furthering the above goals allows one more **Bureaucracy** test, assuming the Agents have found a reliable patron in the legitimate British security apparatus. And assuming they can keep him or her alive long enough to see their project through.

INDEX

Access 32
Agency Cover 31
Alvah see Elvis
Archivist 90
Balogun, David 83, see also Phlebotomist
Barrow, Courtney 91, see also Logistical Support Co-ordinator
Basic Logistical Support 32
Bucharest Night Club Owner 94
Bureaucracy **32**, benefits 33-36
Campaign frame see Fields of Edom
Canter, Maggie 96 see also Church Scavenger
Car gadgets 71
Chain Home Deep 46
Chaudri, Neela 101 see also Social Worker
Church Scavenger 96
Churchill, Winston 53
Ciocan, Sandu 94 see also Bucharest Night Club Owner
Counter-SBA Operations 19
Counterterrorism Operations 8
Creating Edom Agents 28
Cretch, Mrs. 92 see also Secretary
Crossbow 37
Document 1000 see E Squadron Special Assignment Briefing
Document 2000 see Counterterrorism Operations
Document 2100 see Seward Serum
Document 2200 see SBA Escort
Document 2300 see SBA Verification
Document 2400 see Field Precautions
Document 3000 see Counter-SBA Operations
Dukes of Edom **64-81**; as patrons 30; bureaucracy benefits 32-36
Dracula **51**, bargain with 61
Earthquake Damage 42
Earthquake Device man-portable 40; vehicle-mounted 41
Earthquake Technician 81
Edom **25**; building 58; bureaucracy 32-36; creating agents 28; Dukes **64-81**; equipment 36; history 49; lexicon 26; maneuvers 47; org chart 23; redemption 111; scientific staff 81; support staff 90; szohordoks 90; tradecraft 46-47; weapons 37
Edom Blaze (Edom Flash) 46
Edom's Vampire 51
Elah see Oakes
Elvis (Alvah) **64**; as patron 30; bureaucracy benefits 32
Equipment 36
E Squadron **7**; Ratings 86; Special Assignment Briefing 7; Standard Loadout 37
Farmer 97
Fennell, Colin 87 see Veteran Rating
Fields of Edom (campaign frame)

103, running the campaign 108
Field Precautions (briefing) 16
Fort (Mibzar) **64;** bureaucracy benefits 33
Future-proofing the Dossier 62
Gabor, Petra 97 see also Farmer
Go-bar 37
Hawkins, Peter 50
Heat 104
History of Edom 49
HMS Prosperpine **7**; ratings 86
Holy Relics 39
Hound (Kenaz) **67**; as patron 30; bureaucracy benefits 33
Hunting the Dossier 103
Ian (Iram) **69**; bureaucracy benefits 34; custom car gadgets 71
Inside scoop 32
IR/E Grenade 37
Iram see Ian
Jetheth see Nails
Kenaz see Hound
Kukri, carbon-fibre 37
Lexicon 26
Logistical Support Co-ordinator 91
Loman, Nicholas 55
Magdiel see Prince
Mason, Dr Sarah 82 see also Pathologist
Mibzar see Fort
Mirrored Sunglasses 42
Mole Hunt 55
Montseir 56
Nails (Jetheth) **70**; bureaucracy benefits 34
New Blood 88
Oakes (Elah) **72**; as patron 30; bureaucracy benefits 34
Offermans, Jurgen 100 see also Sailor
Oholibamah see Osprey
Opposition 104
Oppyramid 105
Osprey (Oholibamah) **74**; as patron 30, bureaucracy benefits 35
Packet 12, 43
Pathologist 82
Pearl (Pinon) **83**; bureaucracy benefits 35
Phlebotomist 83
Pinon see Pearl
Poole, Henry 90 see also Archivist
Porton Down 52
Prince (Magdiel) **77**; bureaucracy benefits 35
Quicke, Graham 81, see also Earthquake Technician
Ratings, HMS Proserpine 86 see also E Squadron
Research Operations Org Chart 23
Romanian Mortician 99
S-Serum see Seward Serum
Sailor 100

SBA (Special Biological Asset) **12**; container 43; countermeasures 19; escort 12; field precautions 16; verification 14
Scientific Staff 81
Secretary 92
Serum Researcher 84
Seward Serum **43**; briefing 10
Skarlet, Dimitra 99 see also Romanian Mortician
Sinclair, Captain Mark 86 see also Squad Leader
Social Worker 101
Special Biological Asset see SBA
Special Edom Manoeuvres **47**; Active Evasion Tactics 47; Friend In Deed 47; Rat Saw Nothing 47
Squad Leader 86
Stake Tube 44
Stalwart characters 64
Standard Loadout 37
Support Staff 90
Sykes, Dr. Ian 84, see also Serum Researcher
Sykes Formula 85
Szohordak 28, 93
Tactical Fact-Finding Benefits **48**;
Targeted Arson 48; Vampire Nights 48; Vampire Season 48; Water Method 48
Tag Team Tactical Benefits **29**; The Blood Is The Life 30; Check to the King 29; Drink From The Cup 29; Follow The Blur 29; Footsteps of Dracula 30; Jolly Raleigh 29; Juice Box 30; King and Country 30; The Knowledge 30; No Maps Of This Country 29; Reptile Fund 29; Seward's Notes 29; Something's Coming Miss Liza 30; Train in Vein 29
Tectonic Weapons **40**; damage 42, using 42
Teman see Tinman
Timnah see Tyler
Tinman (Teman) **78**; bureaucracy benefits 36
Tradecraft 46
Treacherous characters 64
Tyler (Timnah) **79**; as patron 30; bureaucracy benefits 36
Ultraviolet Weapons 38
Unreliable characters 64
UV Dazzle Laser 39
UV Tactical Projector 39
UV Flood Lamp 40
White Serum 45
Wyre, Eric 88
Vampire Tester 45
Vampirology, Edom-Style 28
Veteran Rating 87
Weapons 37
X-ATV-TR 38